W9-CZR-033

Dot-to-Dot
MINDFULNESS

Dot-to-Dot
MINDFULNESS

CHRIS BELL

ARCTURUS

Page 11: This picture is made from 3 continuous lines:
a) numbers 1–313; b) lower case letters a–r; c) upper case
letters A–N.
Page 63: This picture is made from 2 continuous lines:
a) numbers 1–318; b) lower case letters a–z.
Page 83: This picture is made from 2 continuous lines:
a) numbers 1–354; b) lower case letters a–n.
Page 121: This picture is made from 3 continuous lines:
a) numbers 1–419; b) lower case letters a–yyy; c) upper case
letters A–Y.

ARCTURUS

This edition published in 2016 by Arcturus Publishing Limited
26/27 Bickels Yard, 151–153 Bermondsey Street,
London SE1 3HA

Copyright © Arcturus Holdings Limited

All rights reserved. No part of this publication may be reproduced,
stored in a retrieval system, or transmitted, in any form or by any means,
electronic, mechanical, photocopying, recording or otherwise, without
prior written permission in accordance with the provisions of the
Copyright Act 1956 (as amended). Any person or persons who do any
unauthorised act in relation to this publication may be liable to criminal
prosecution and civil claims for damages.

ISBN: 978-1-78599-105-9
CH004810NT

Printed in China

Contents

Introduction

Calming and quietening the mind after a hectic day is important for everyone, and what better way to soothe anxiety and achieve a mindful state than with an activity that massages the brain and helps it focus on the creative things in life. Dot-to-dot is joined-up thinking, in the best possible way. And ahead of you is a wonderful gallery of images to complete.

All that is required is the ability to join consecutively numbered dots using no more than a sharp eye and a sharp pencil. You will need to watch out for numbers that are in sequence but not necessarily next to each other on the page, in which case some careful searching may be required.

Take your time and as you complete each image meditate on what you have done. We hope you will find that the whole process induces calming thoughts and creativity. But first, sharpen your pencil and ease yourself into the book by trying the picture opposite to see how it all works.

Enjoy!

Chris Bell

NB: Some images are made up of more than one continuous line. For a list of these, please go to the notes on page 4.

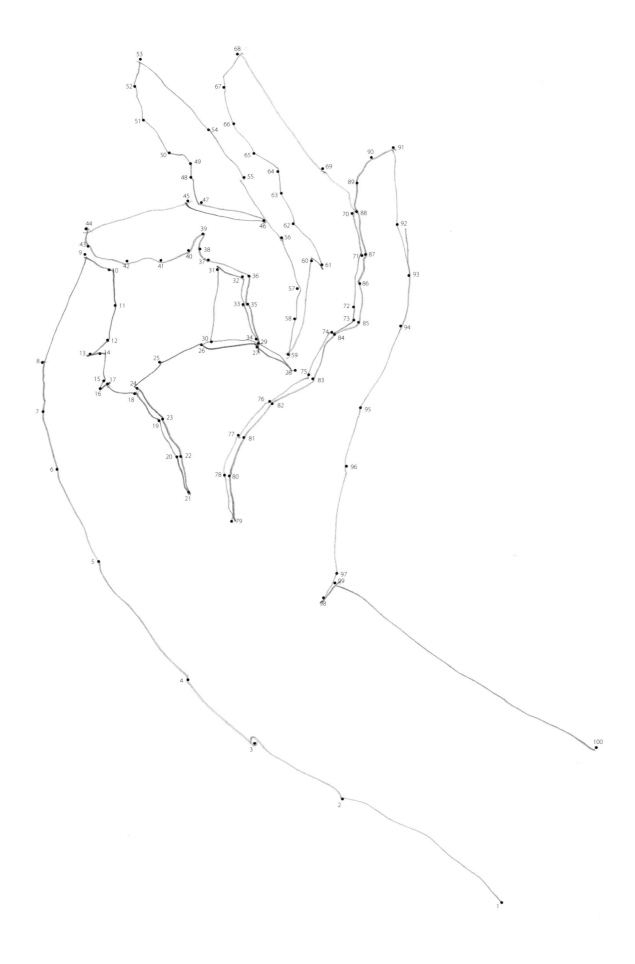

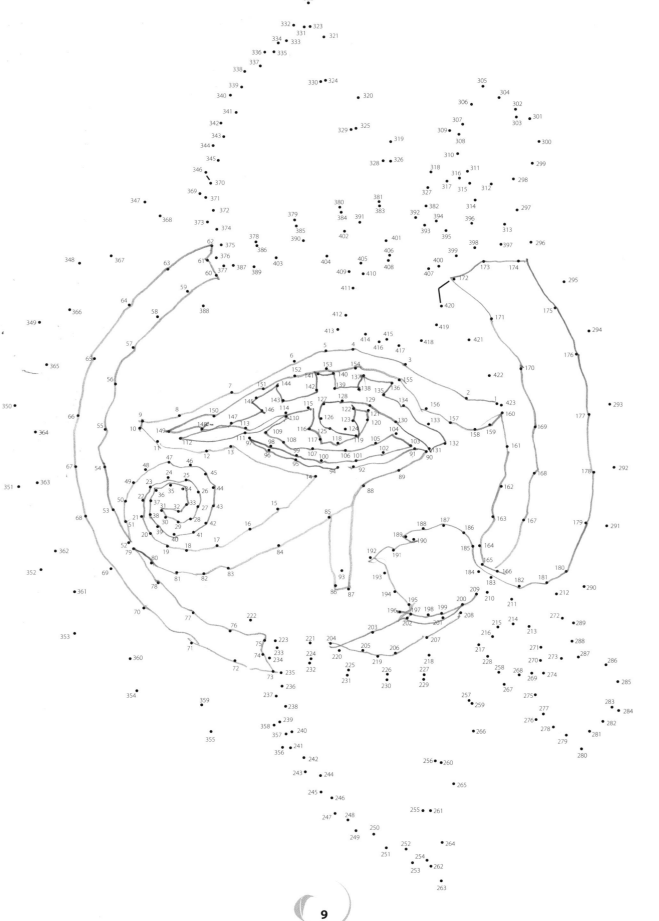

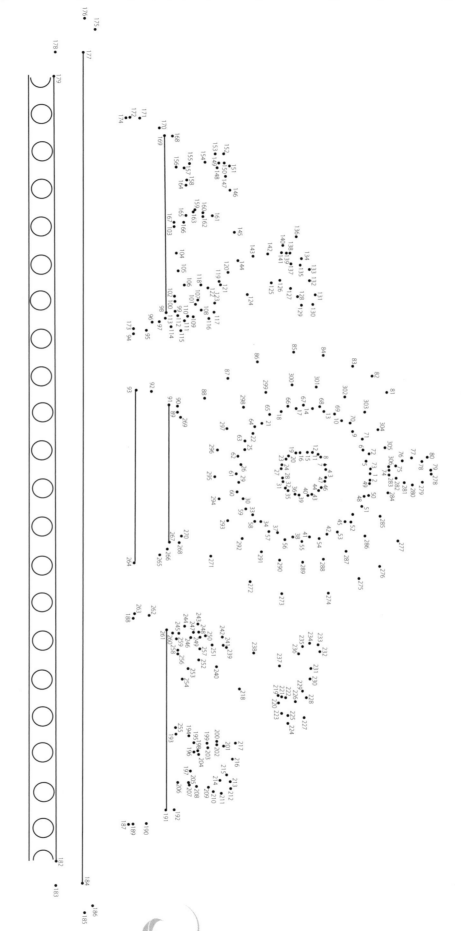

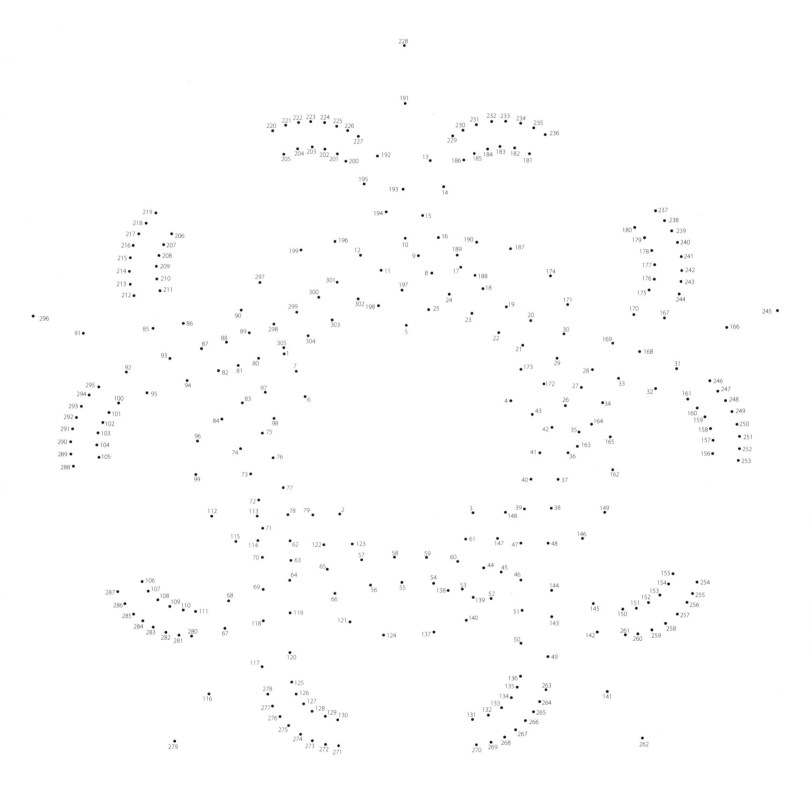

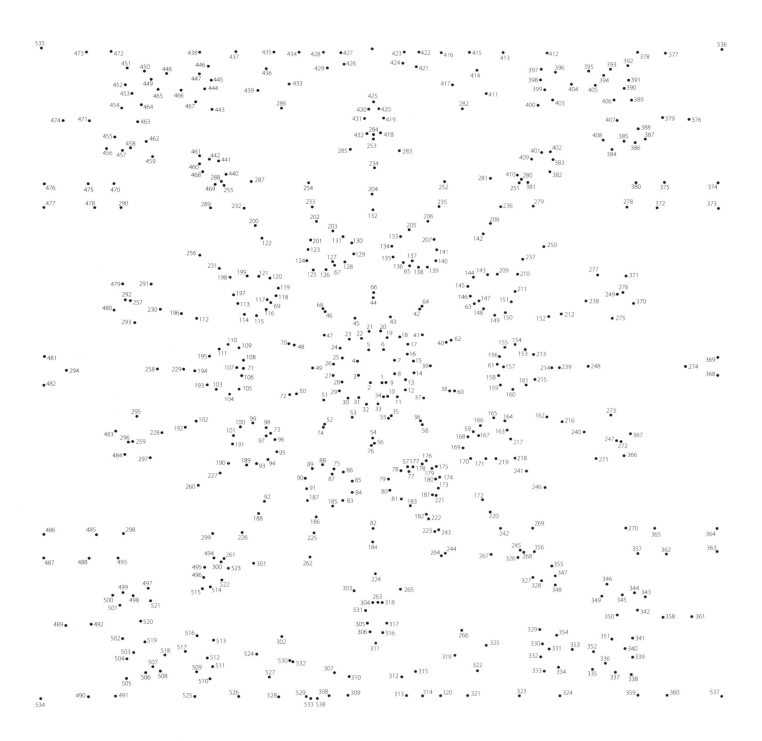

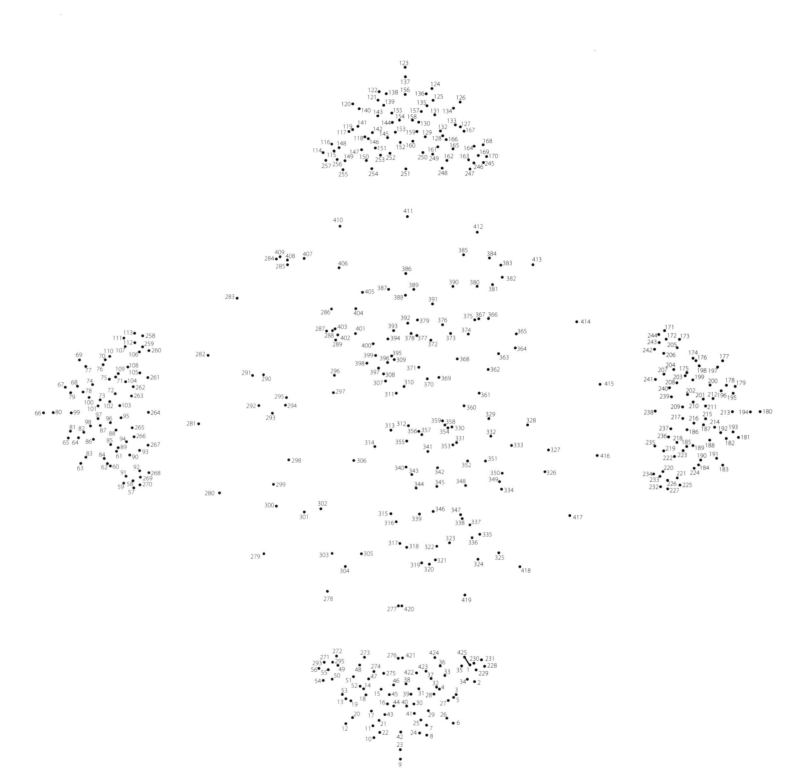

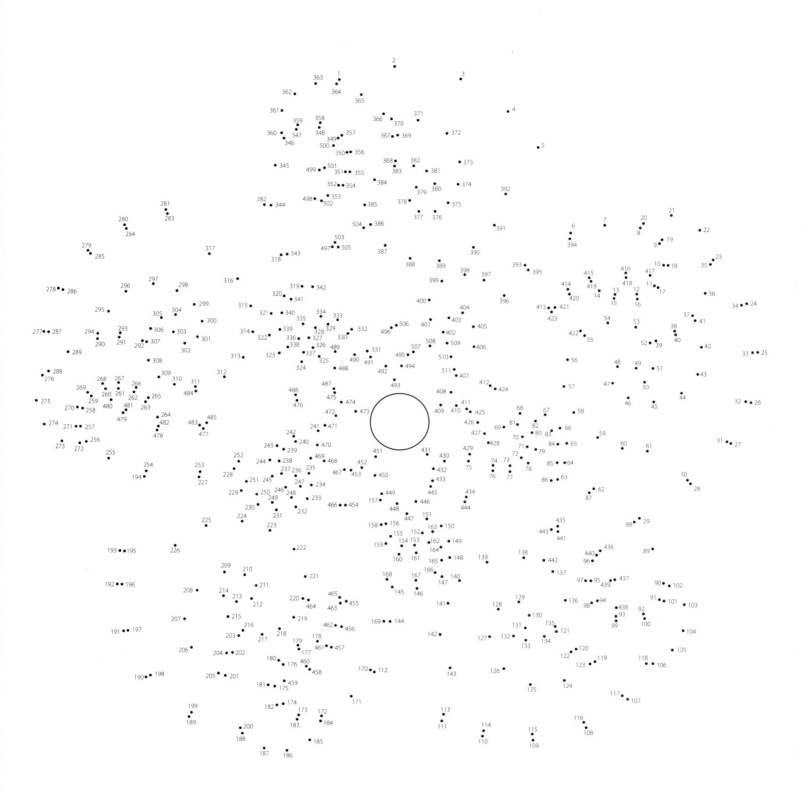

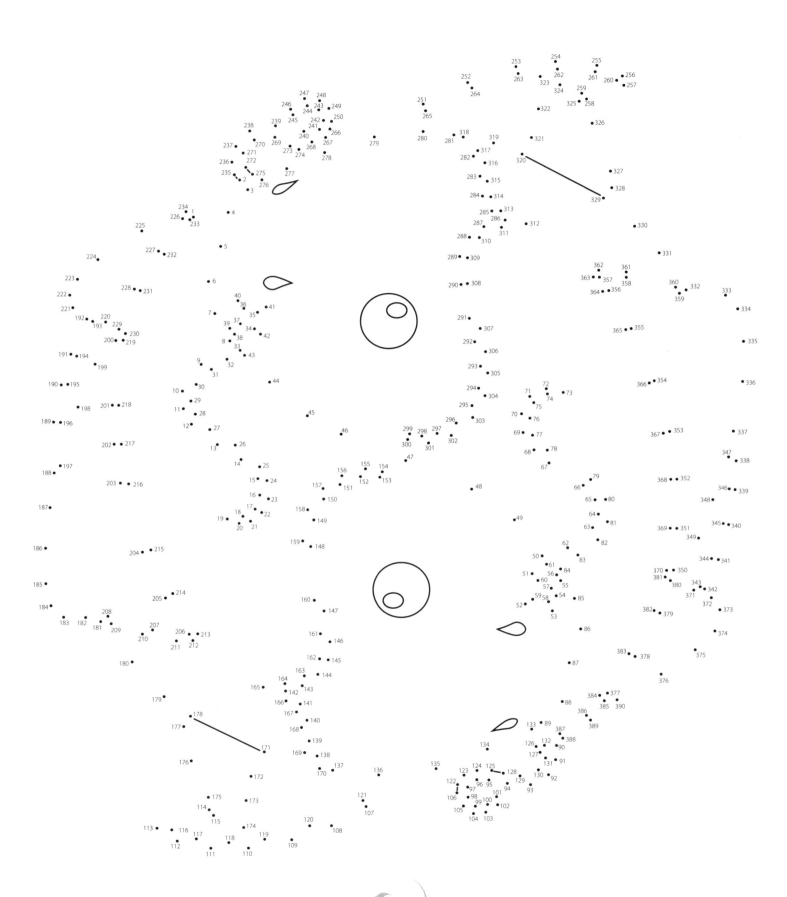

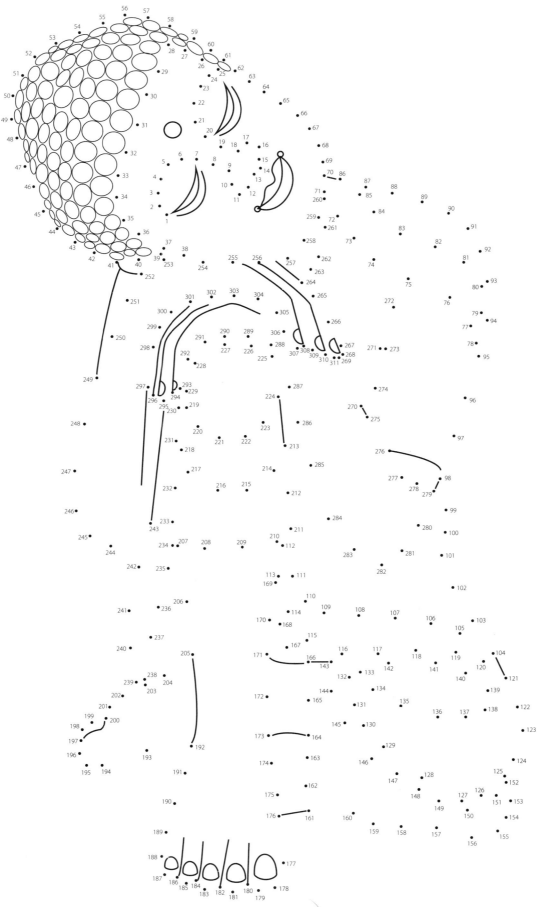

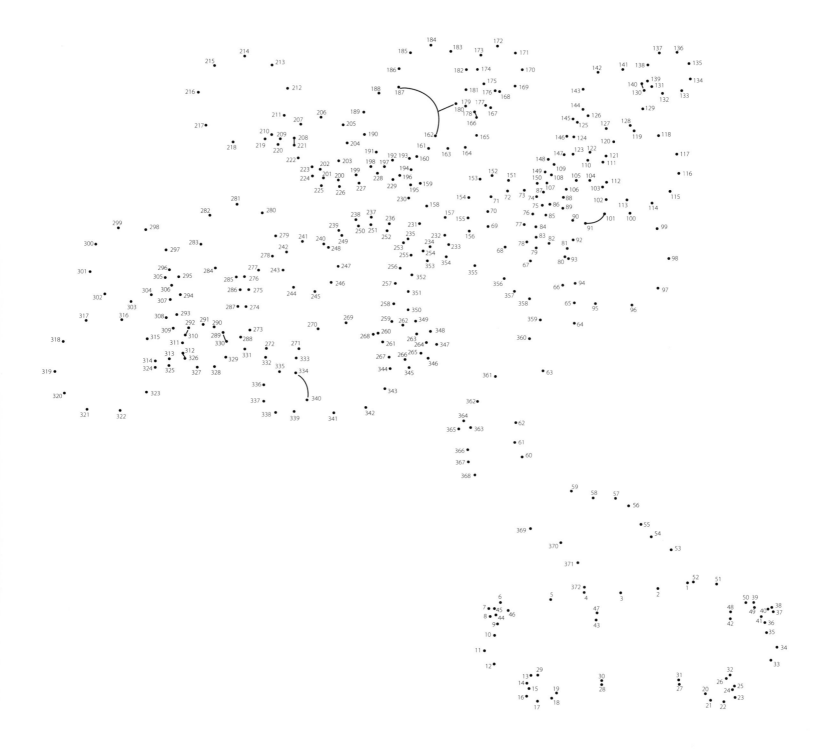

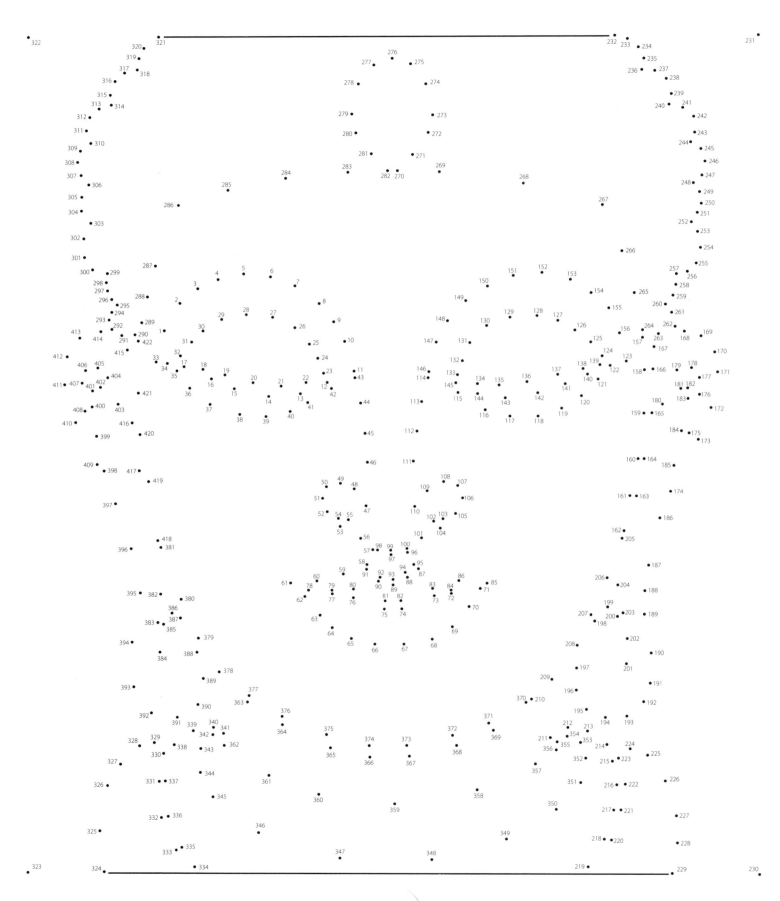

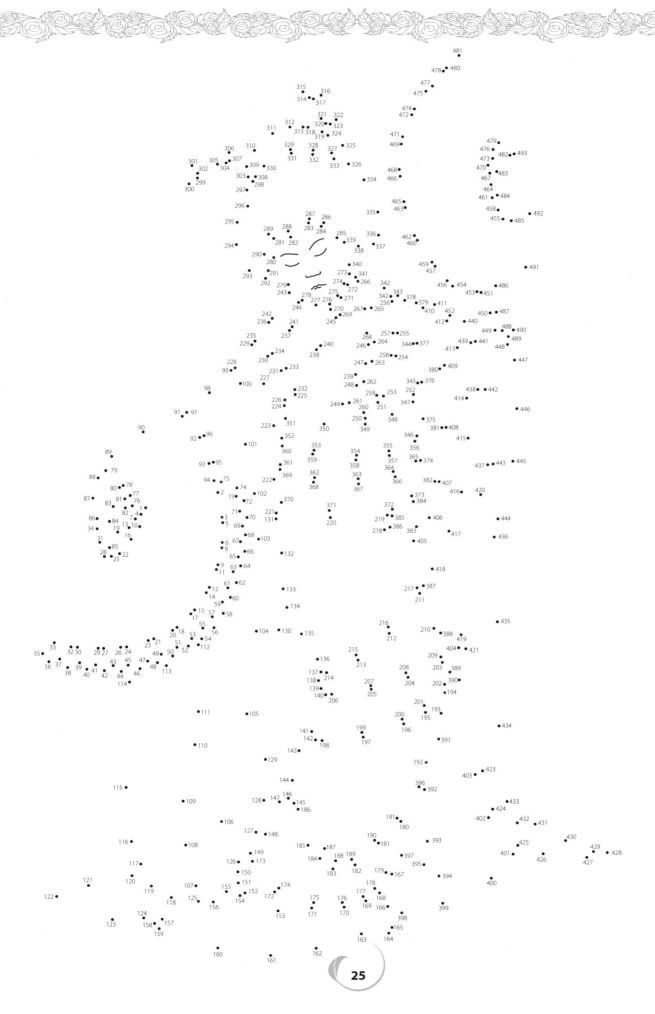

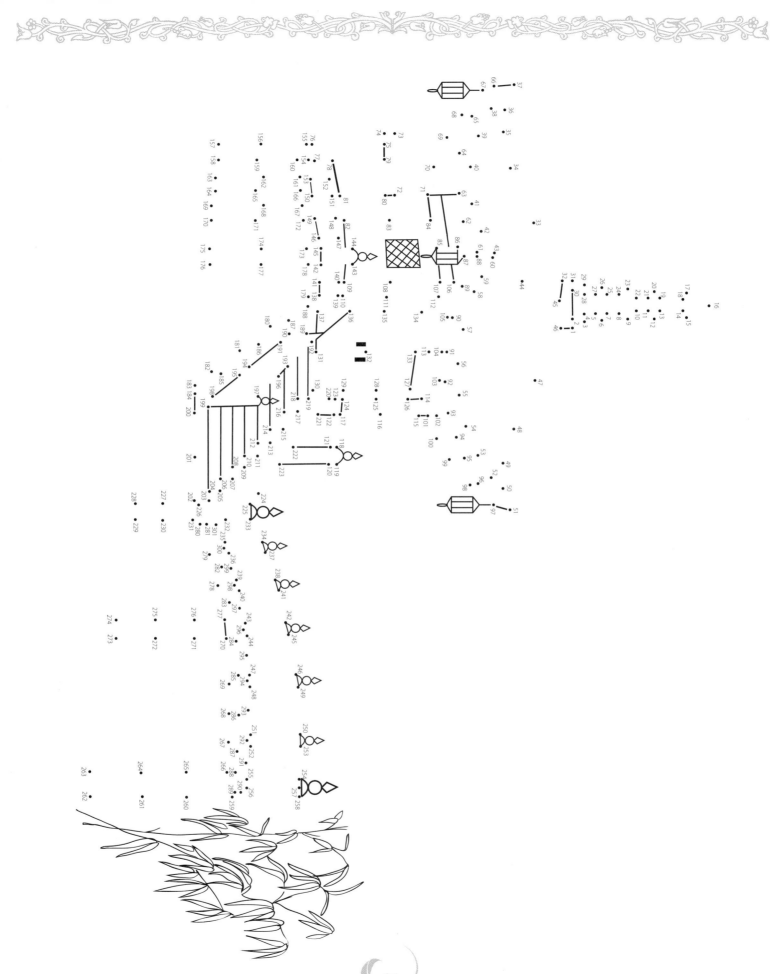

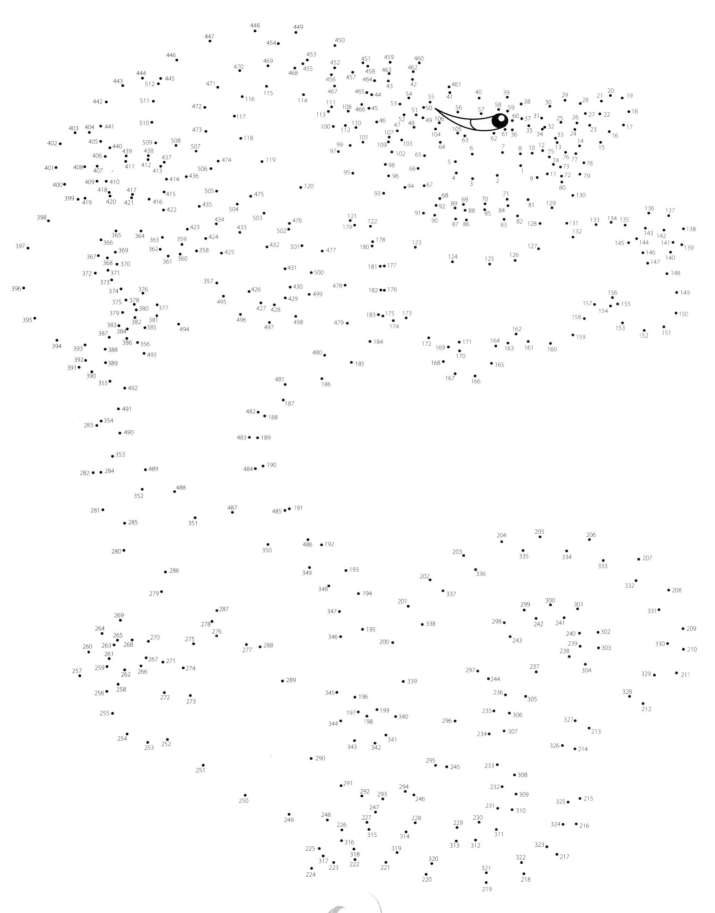

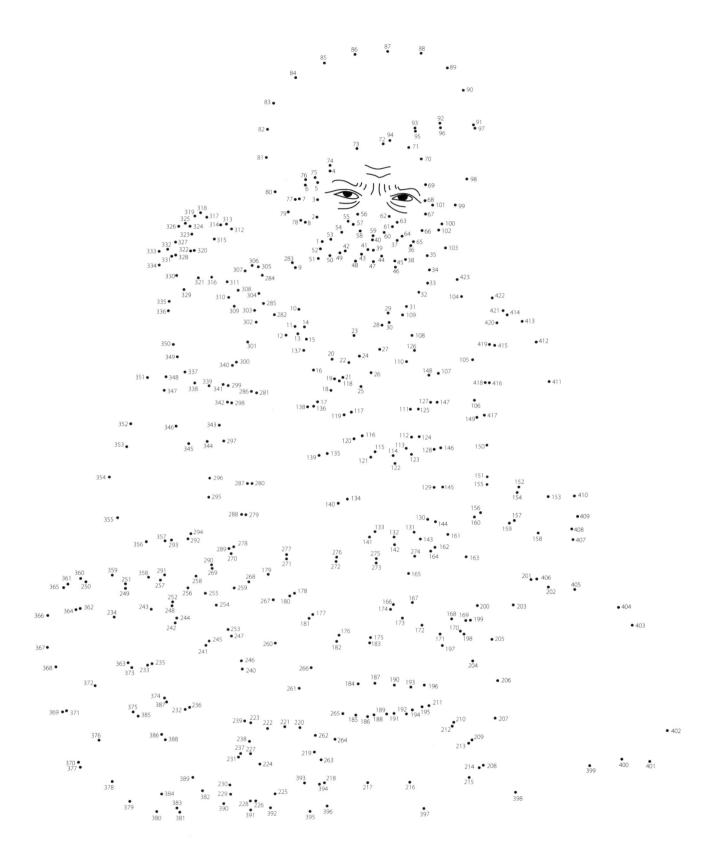

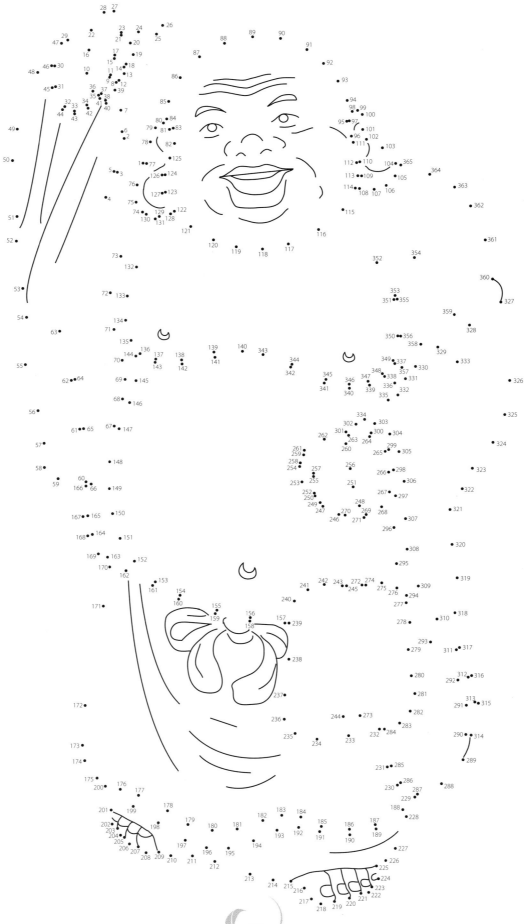

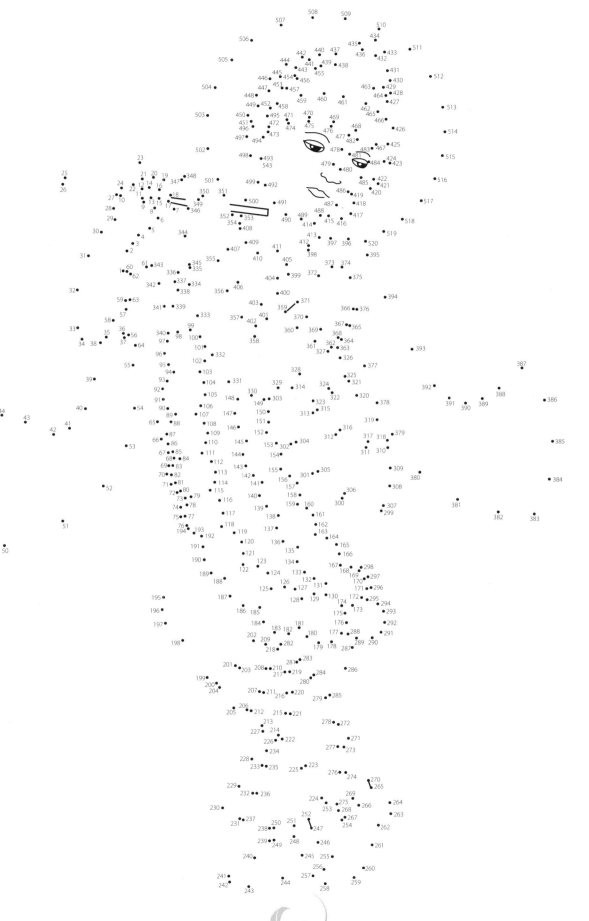

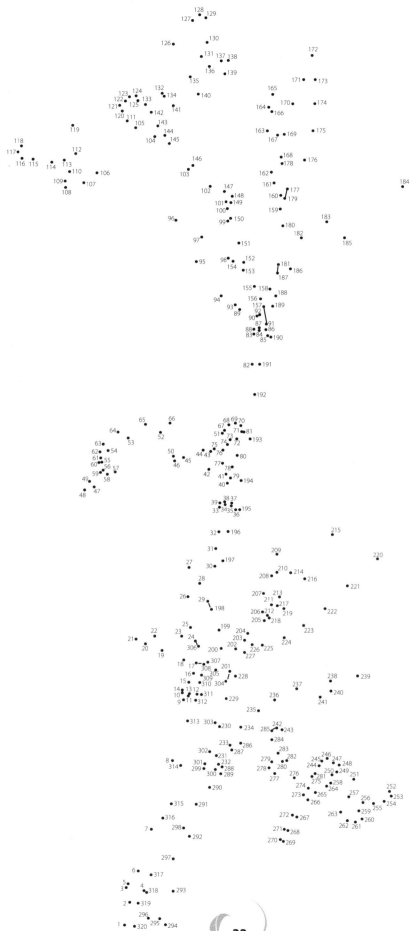

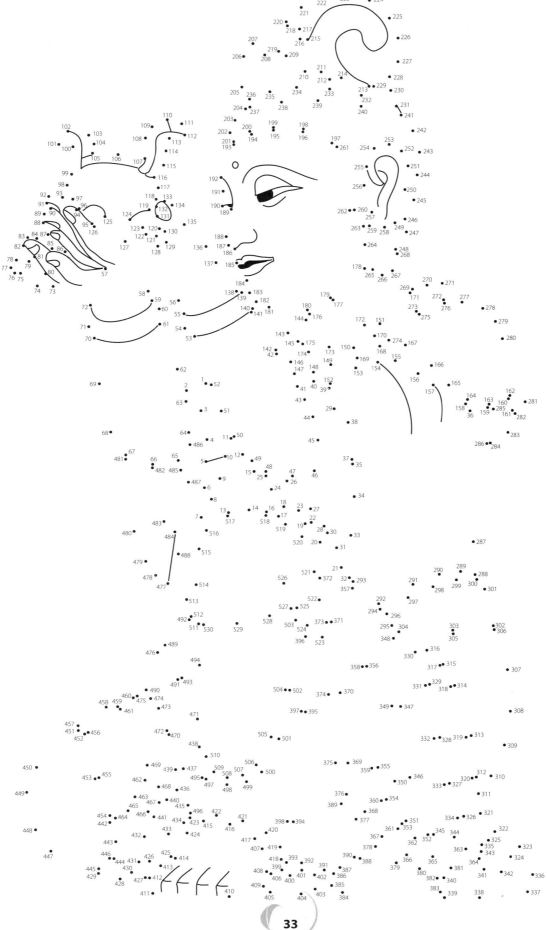

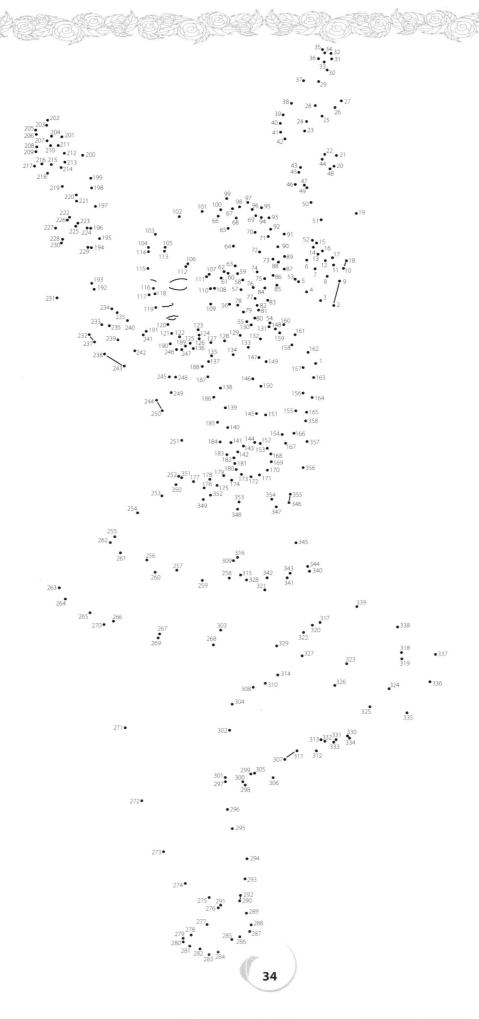

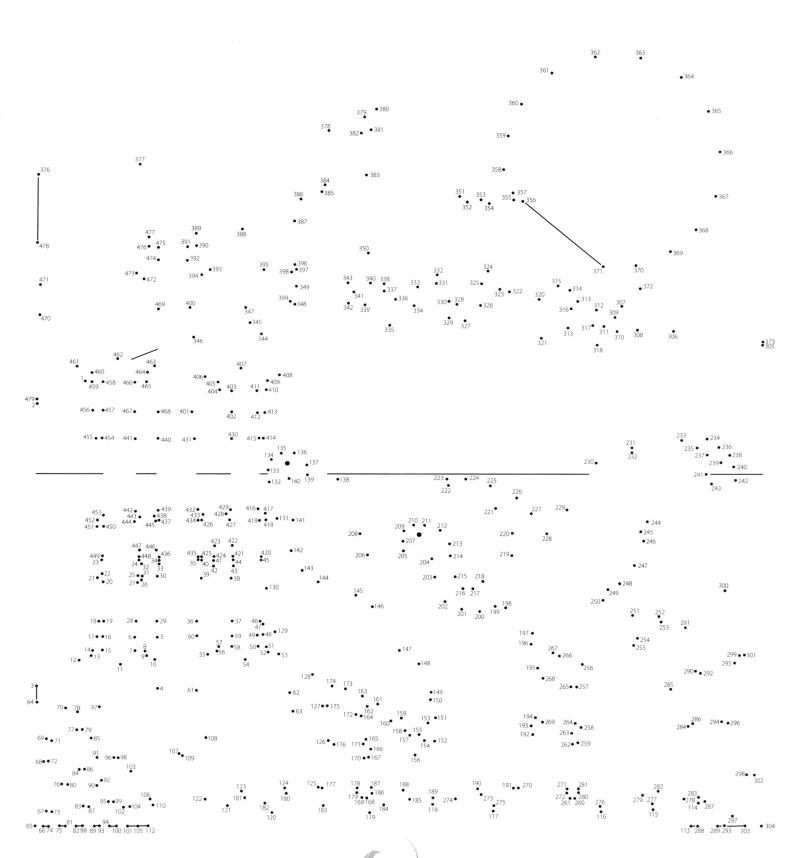

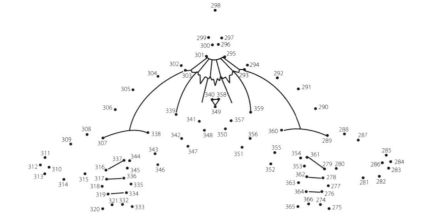
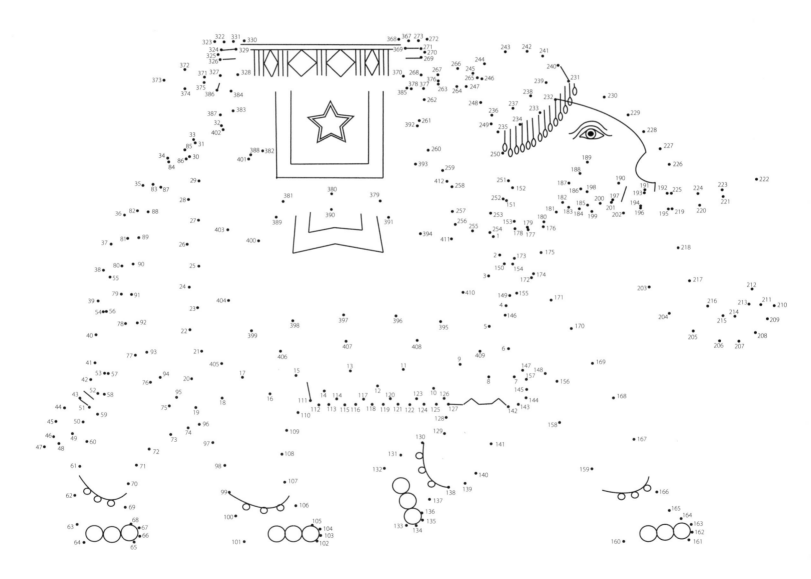

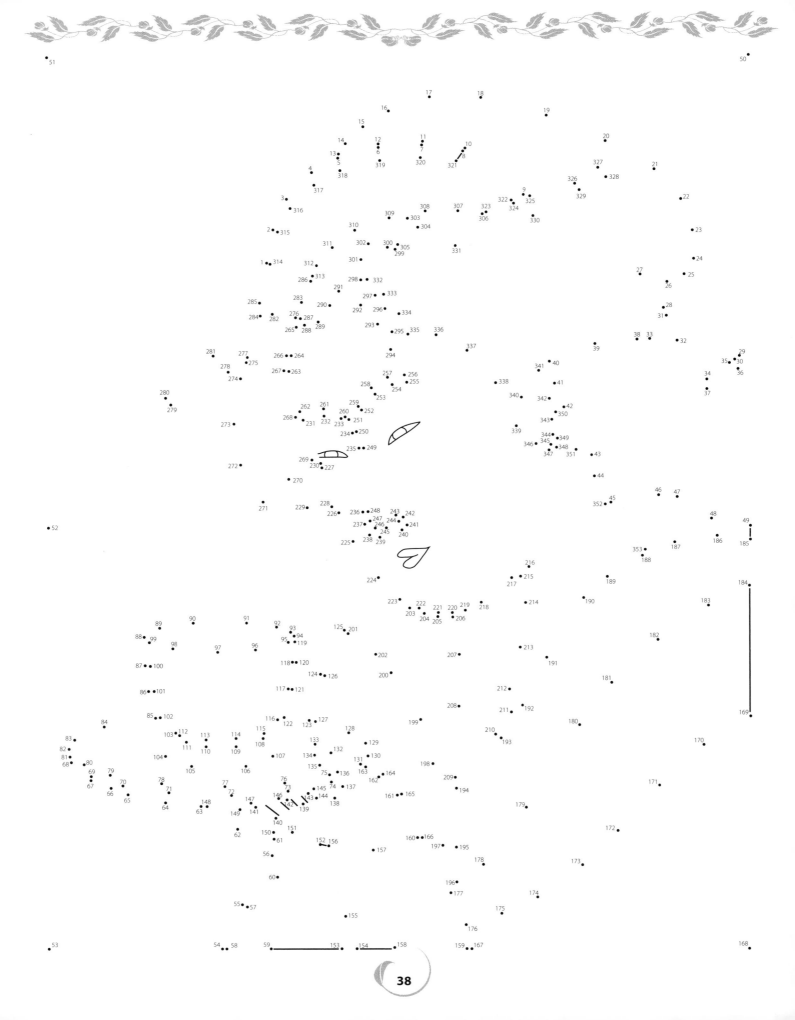

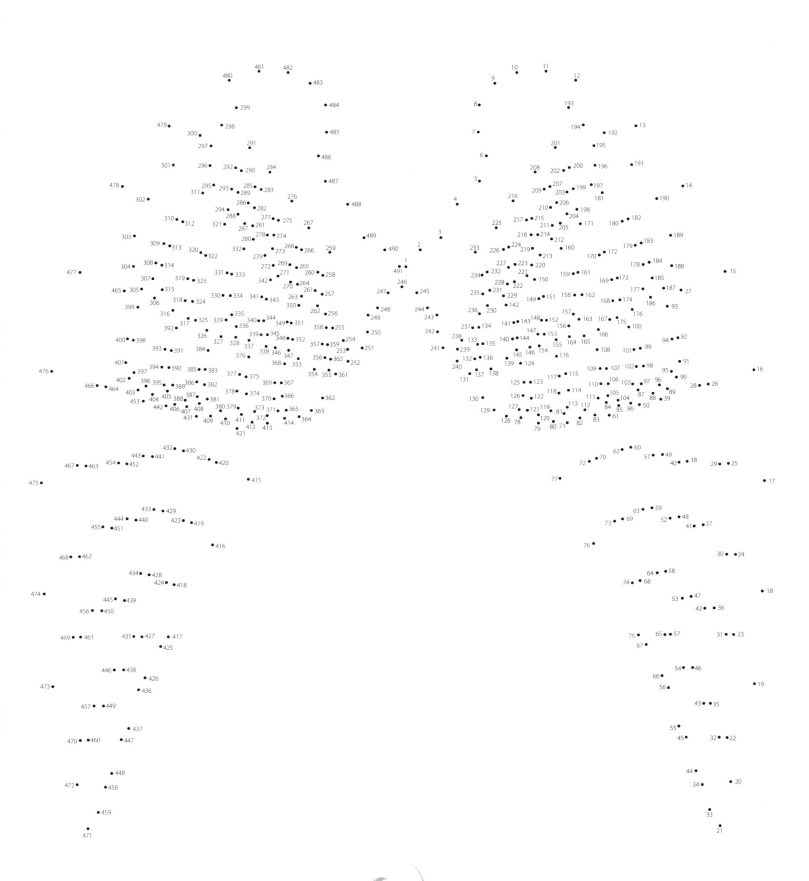

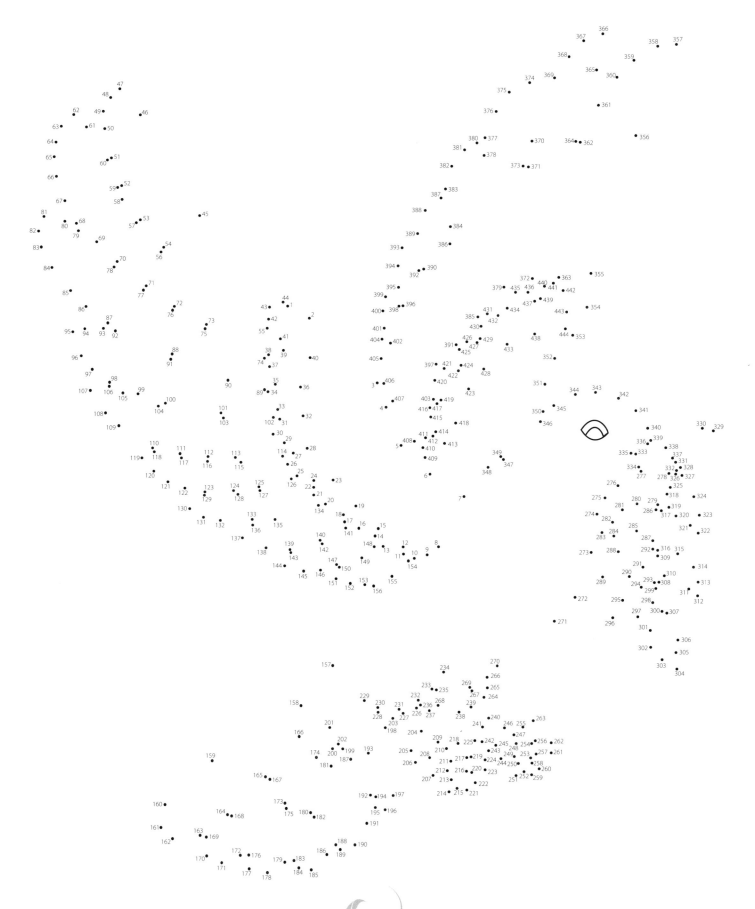

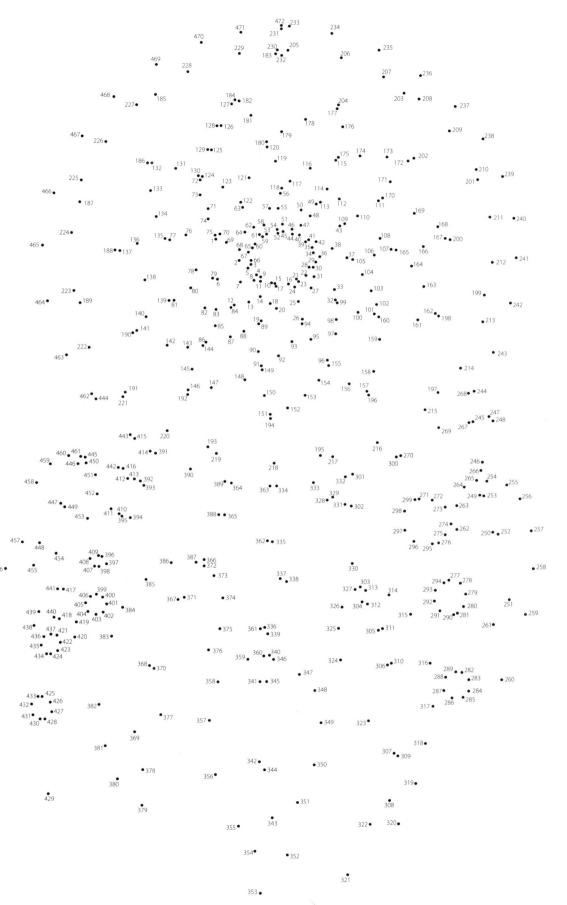

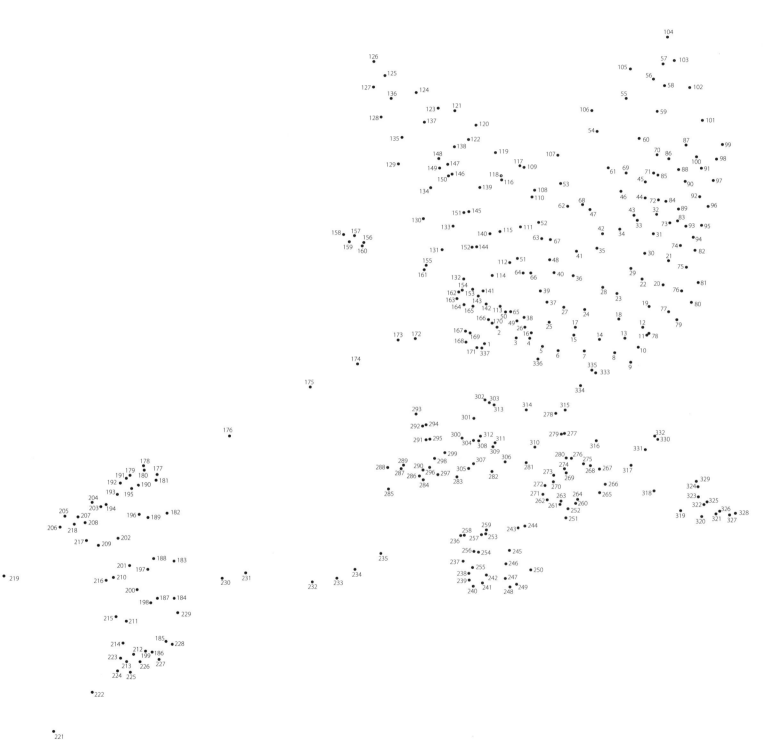

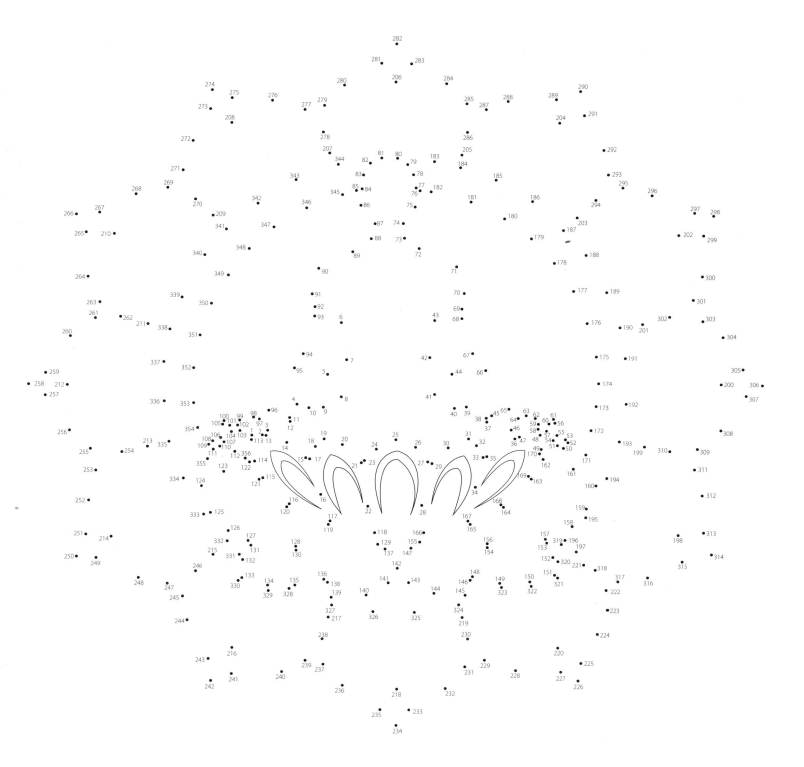

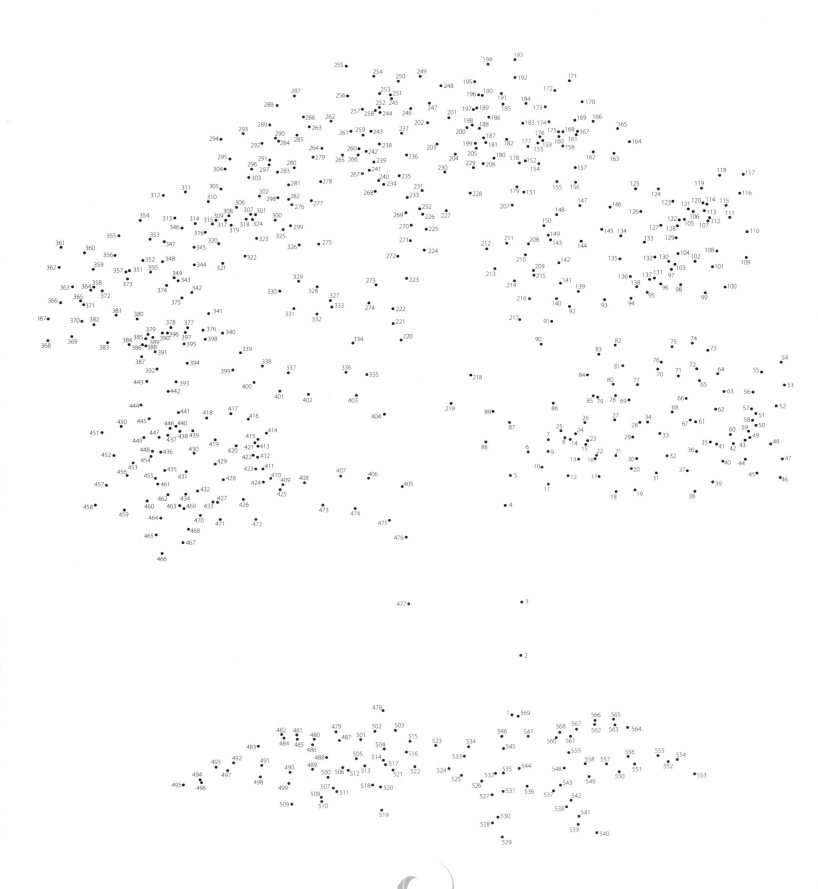

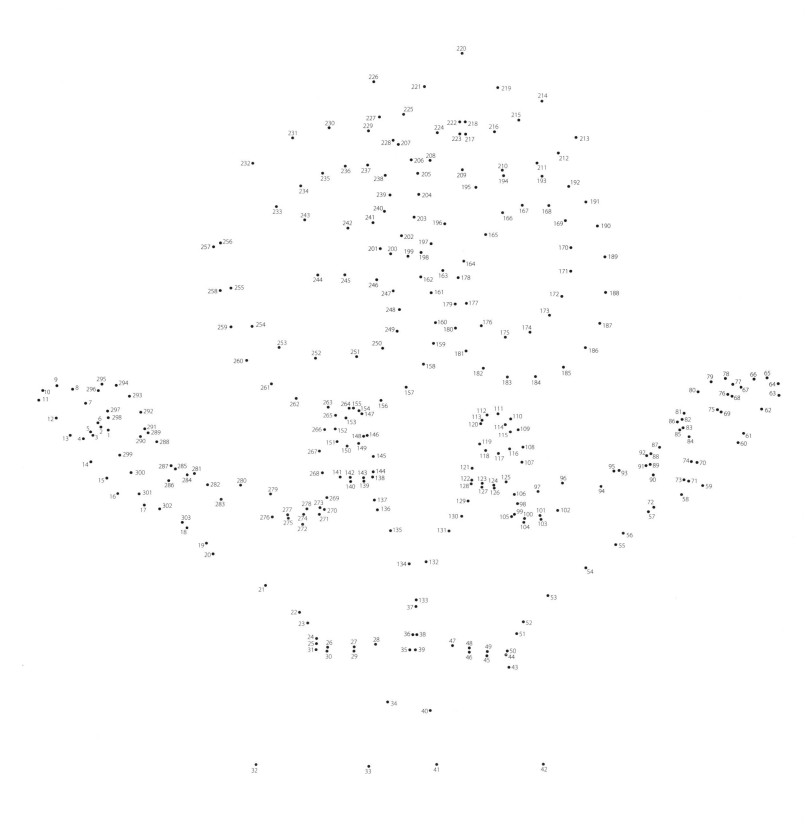

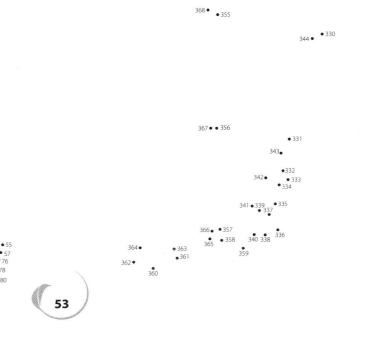

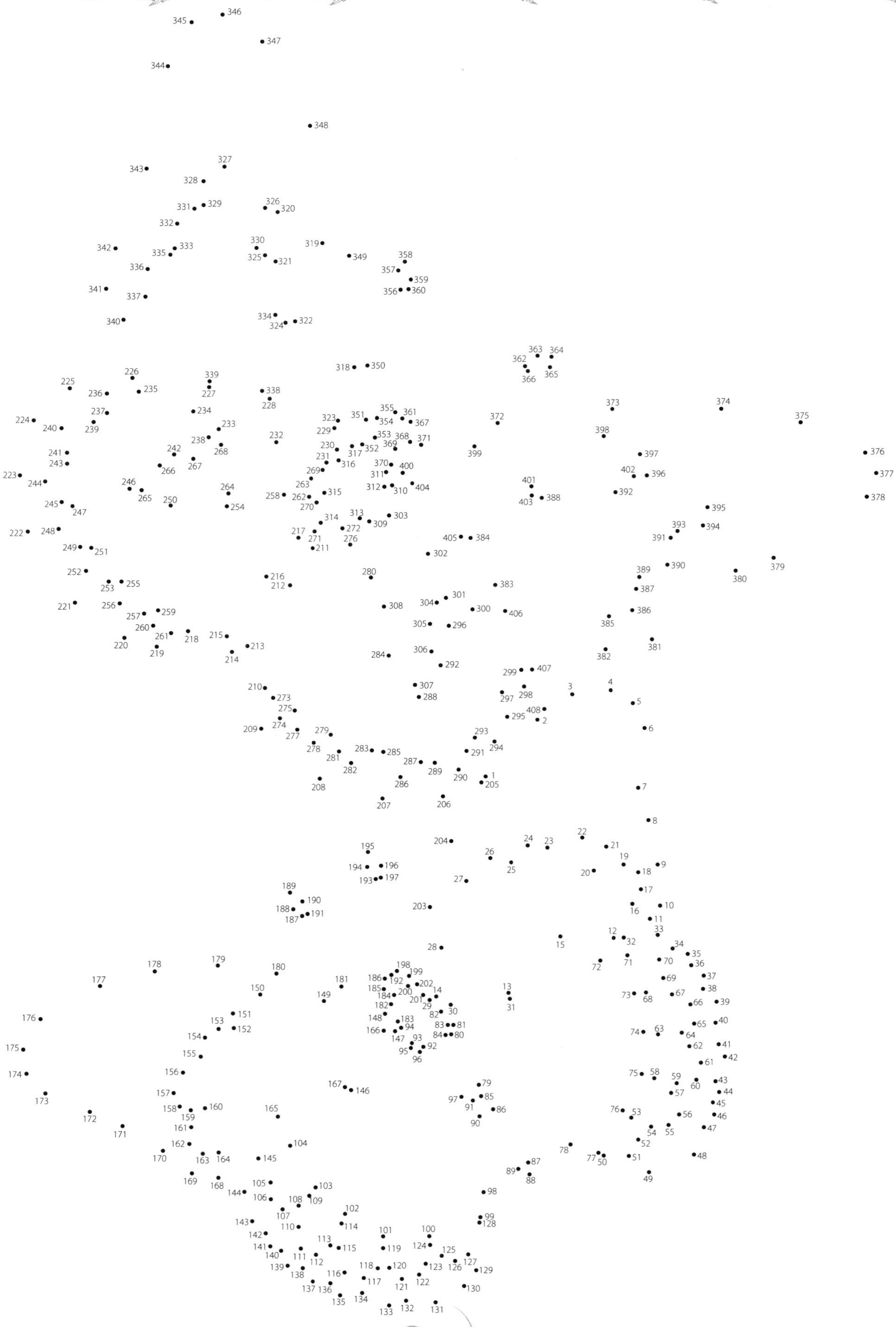

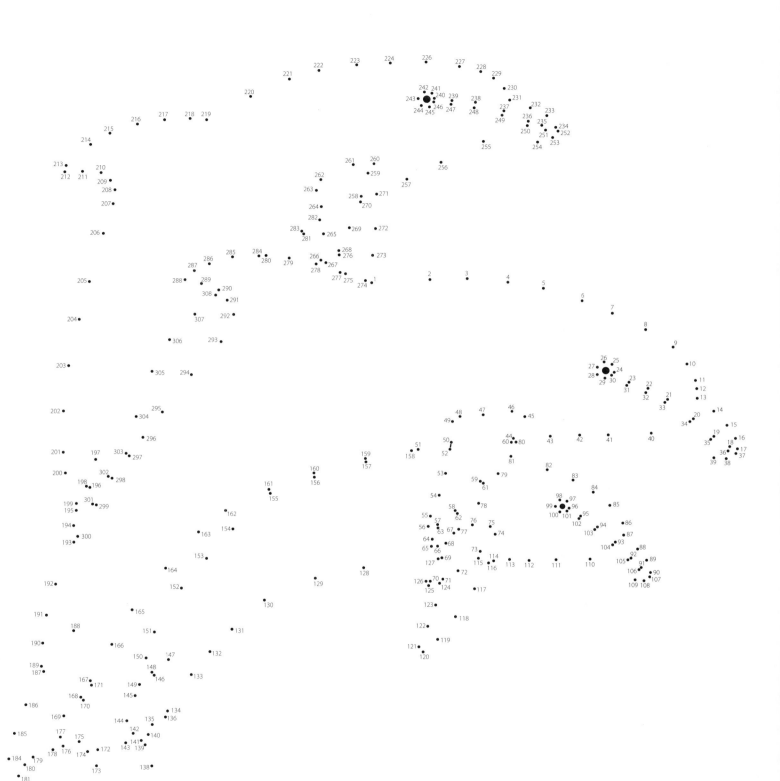

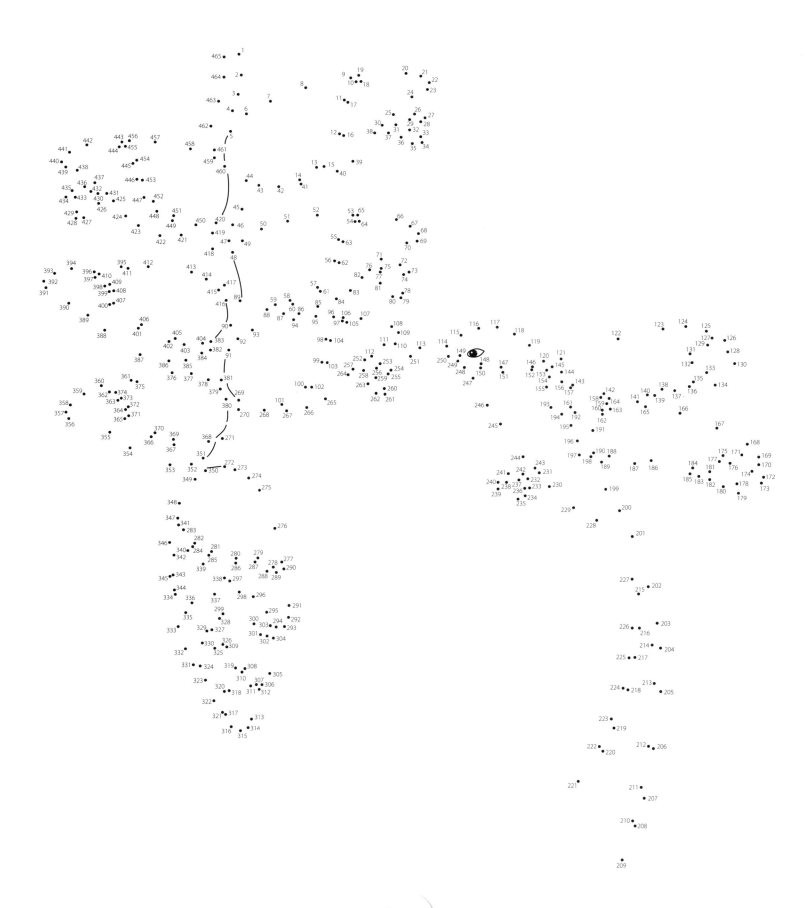

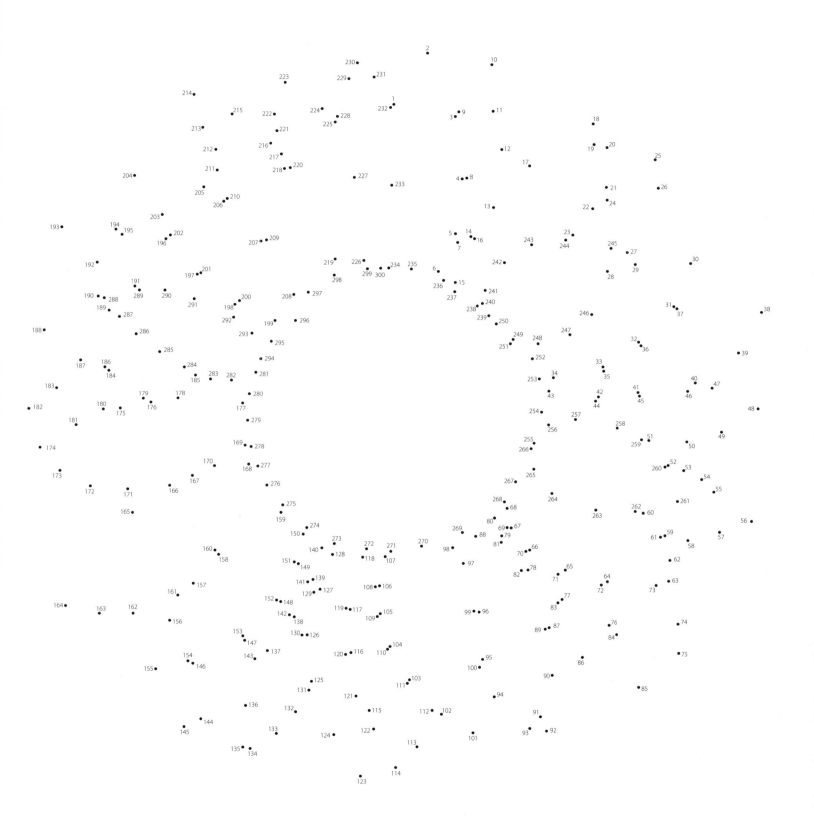

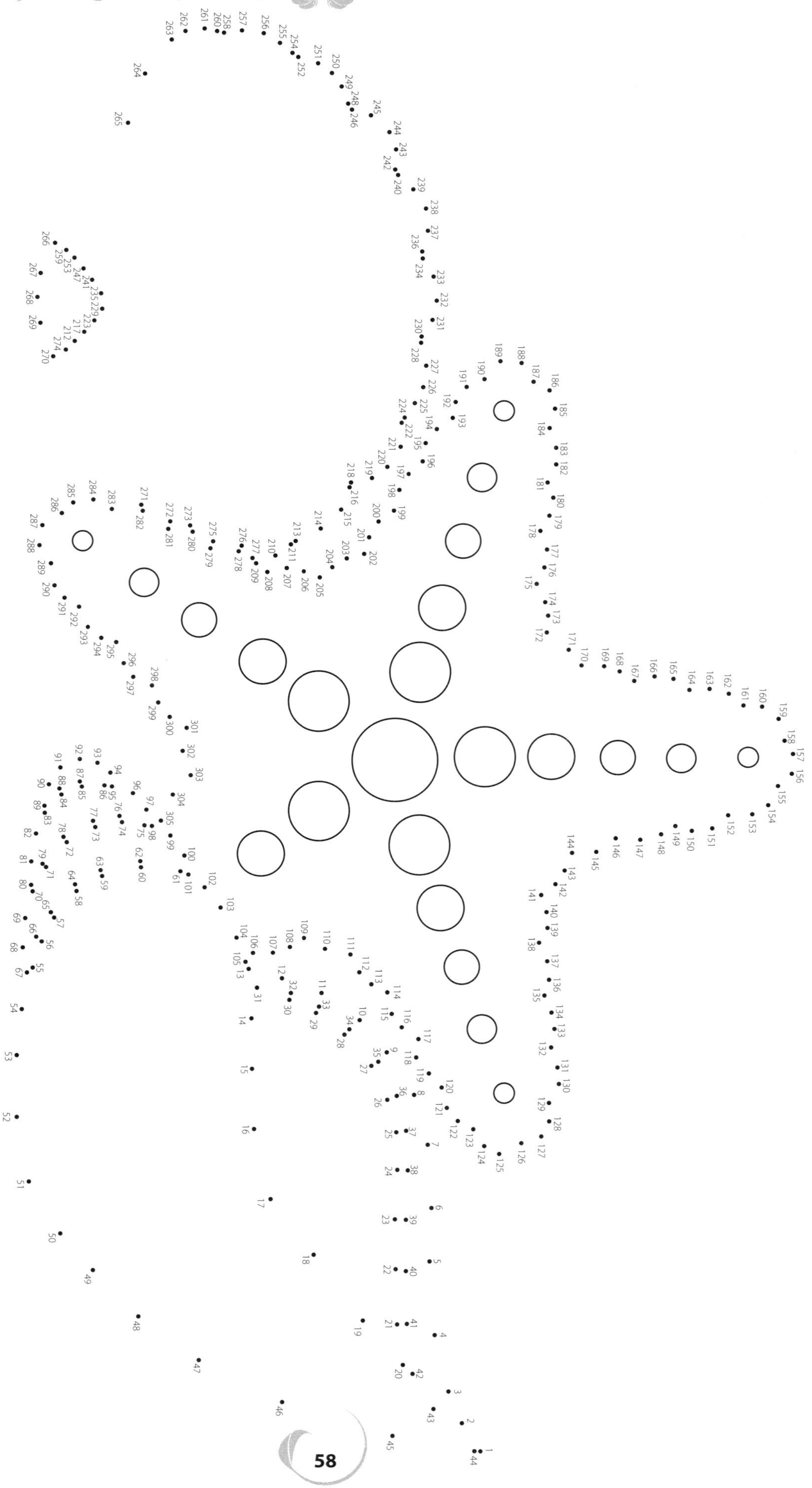

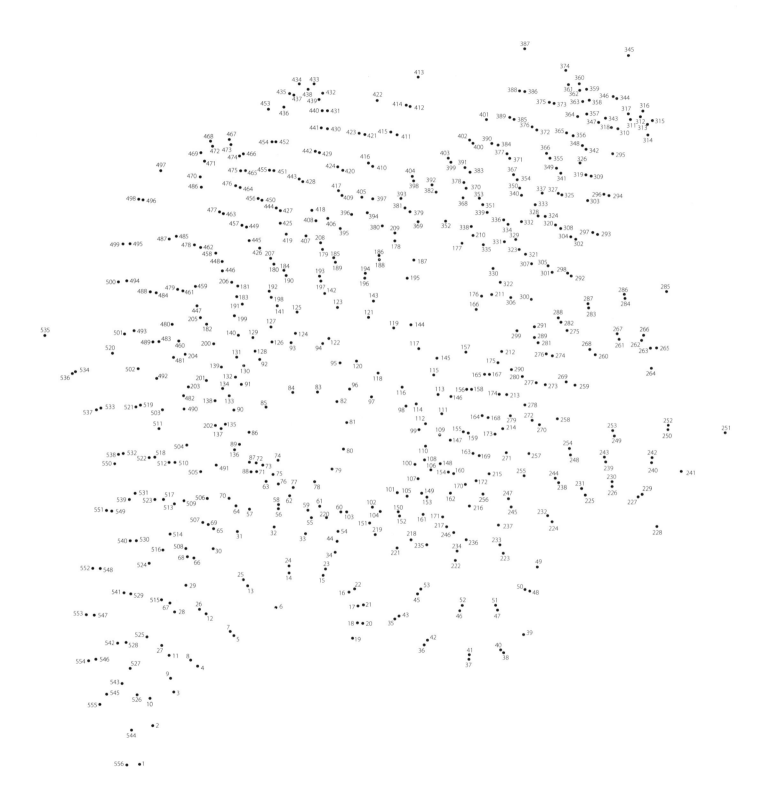

61

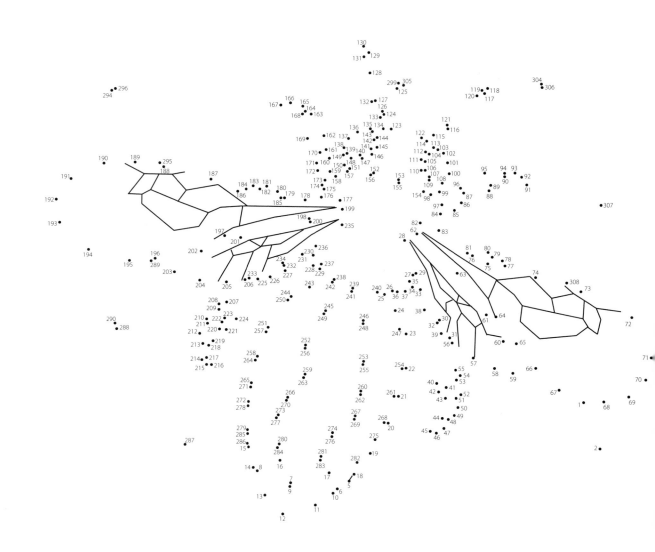

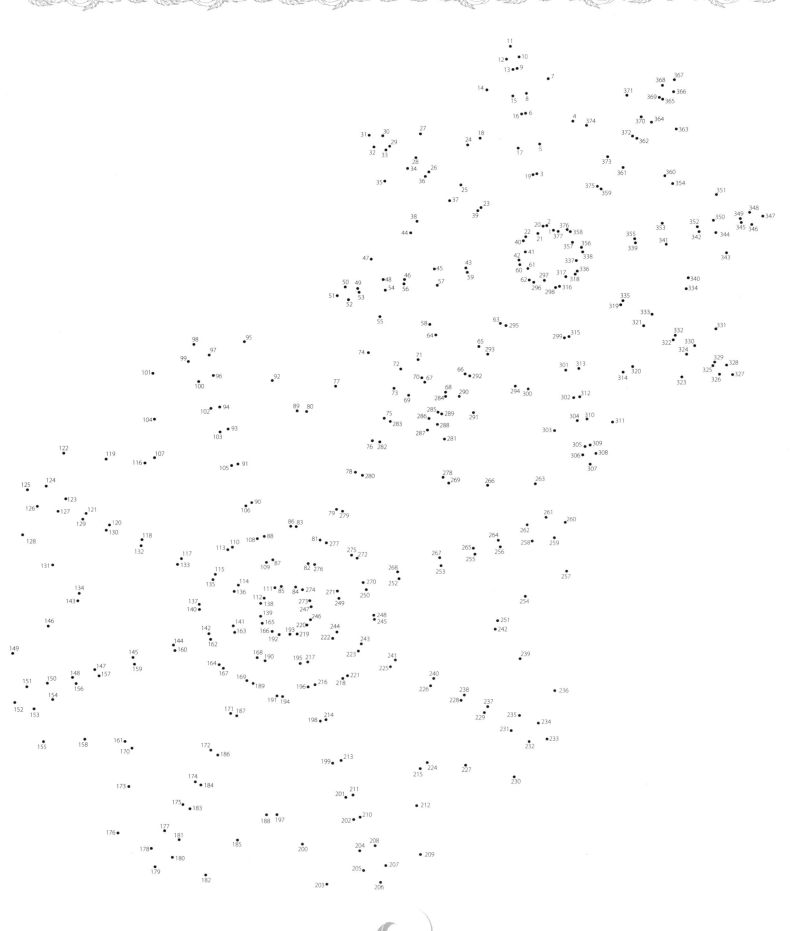

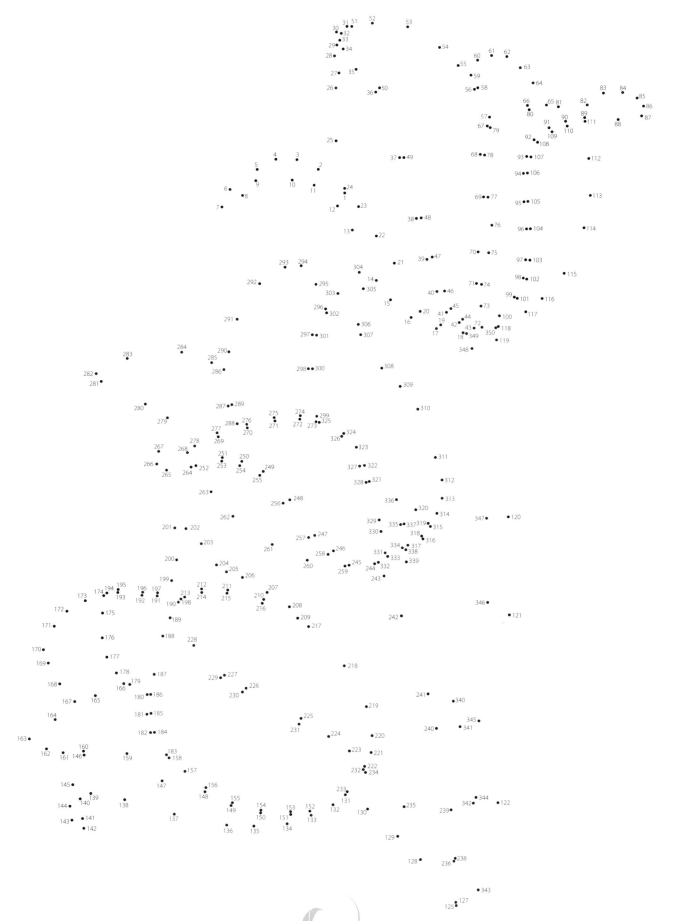

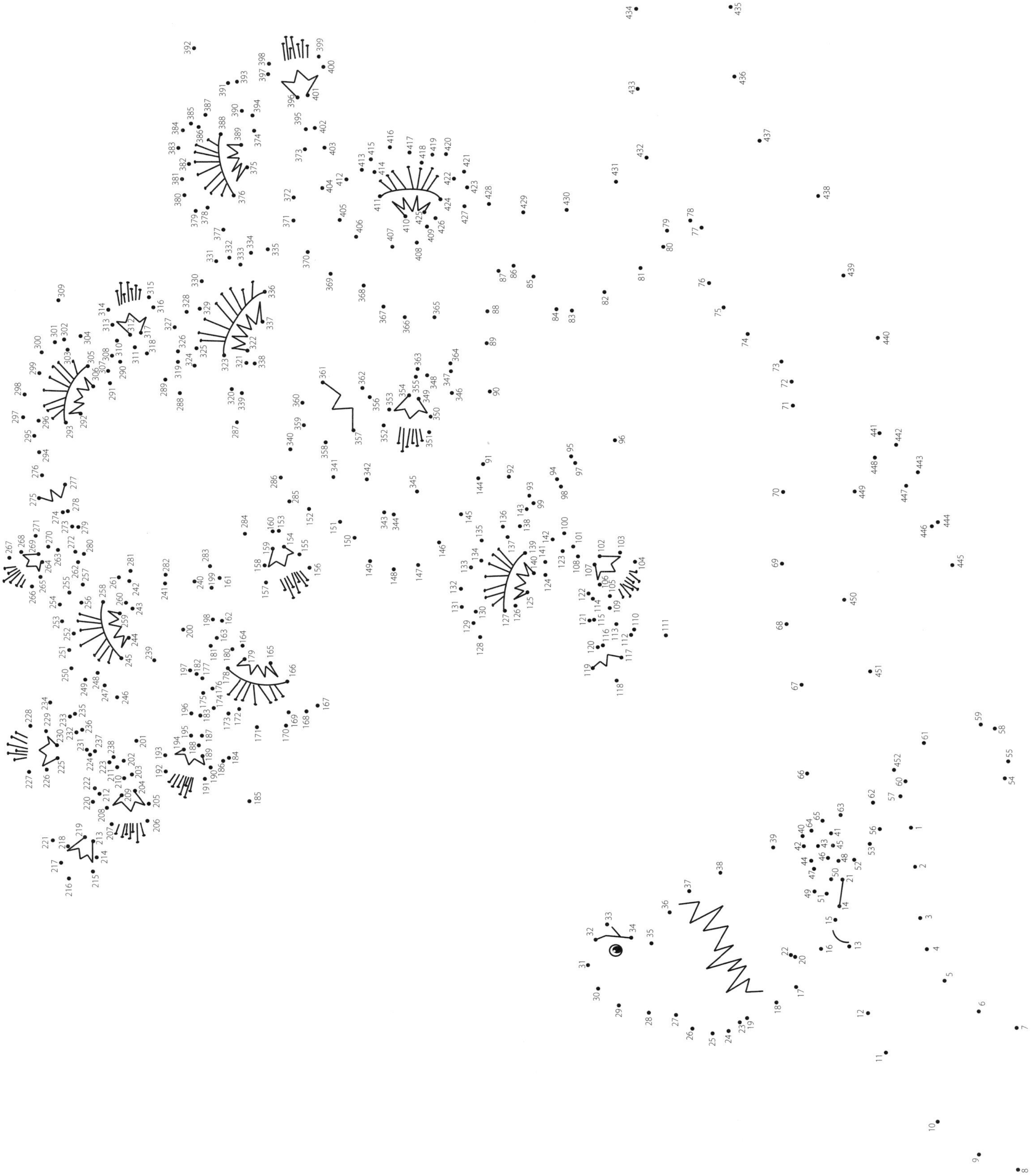

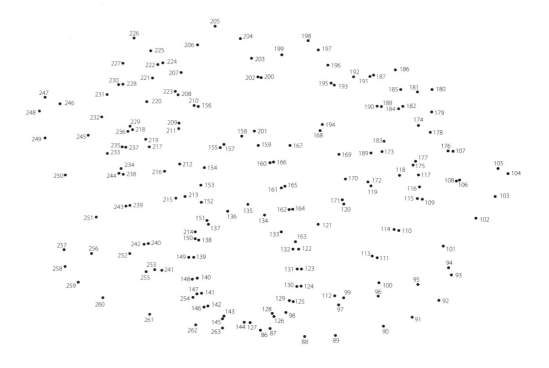

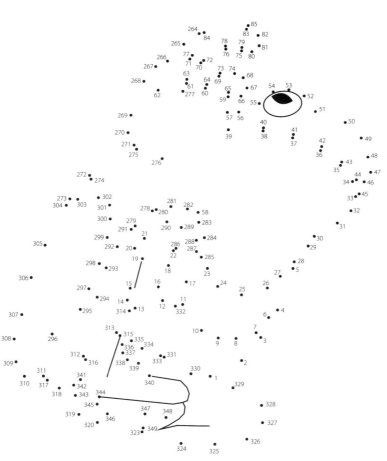

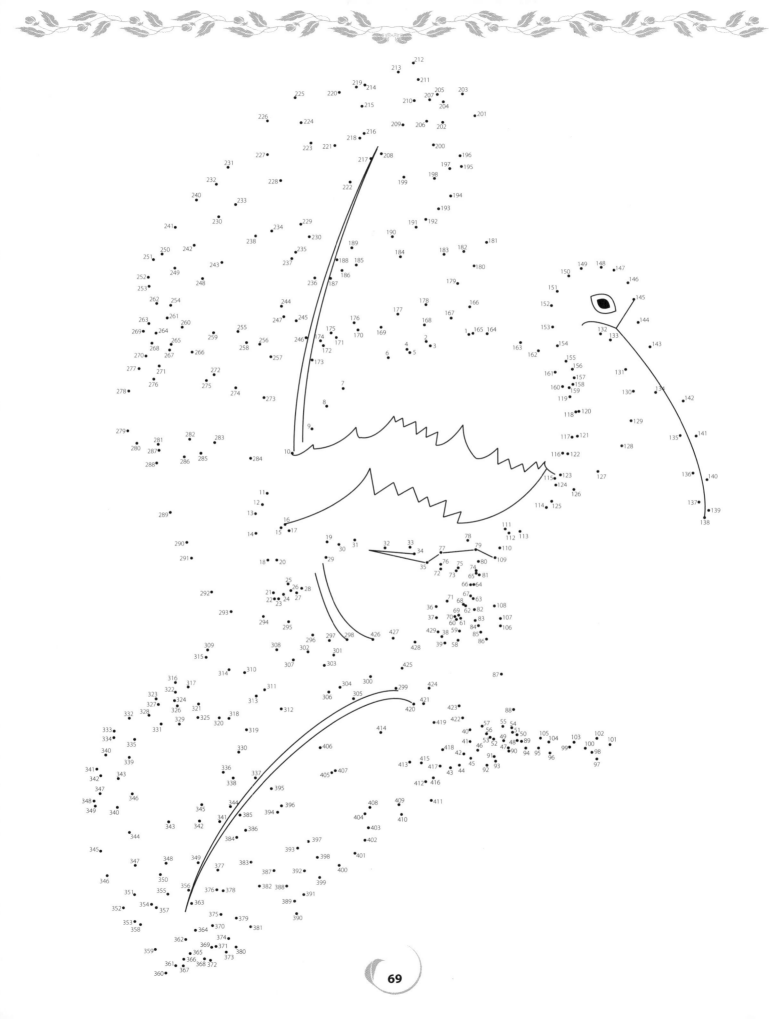

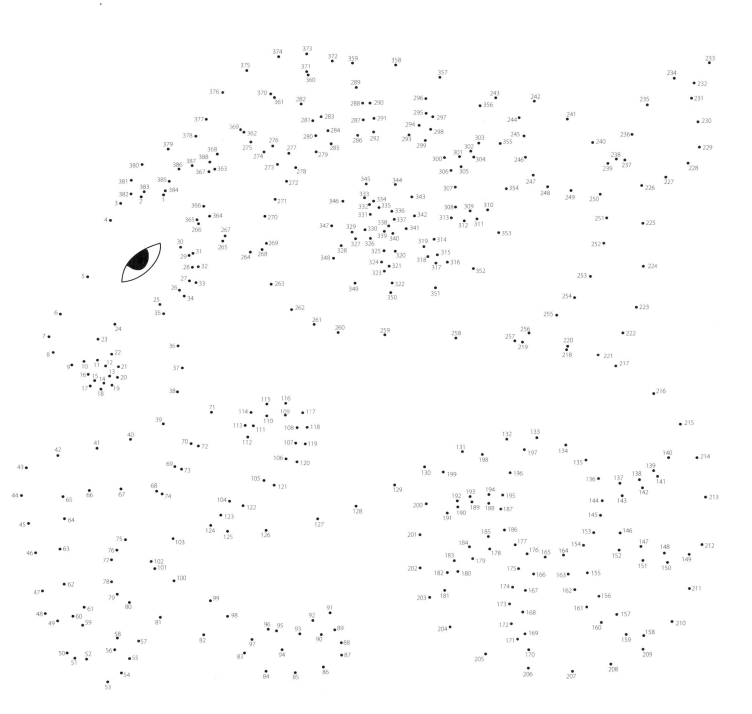

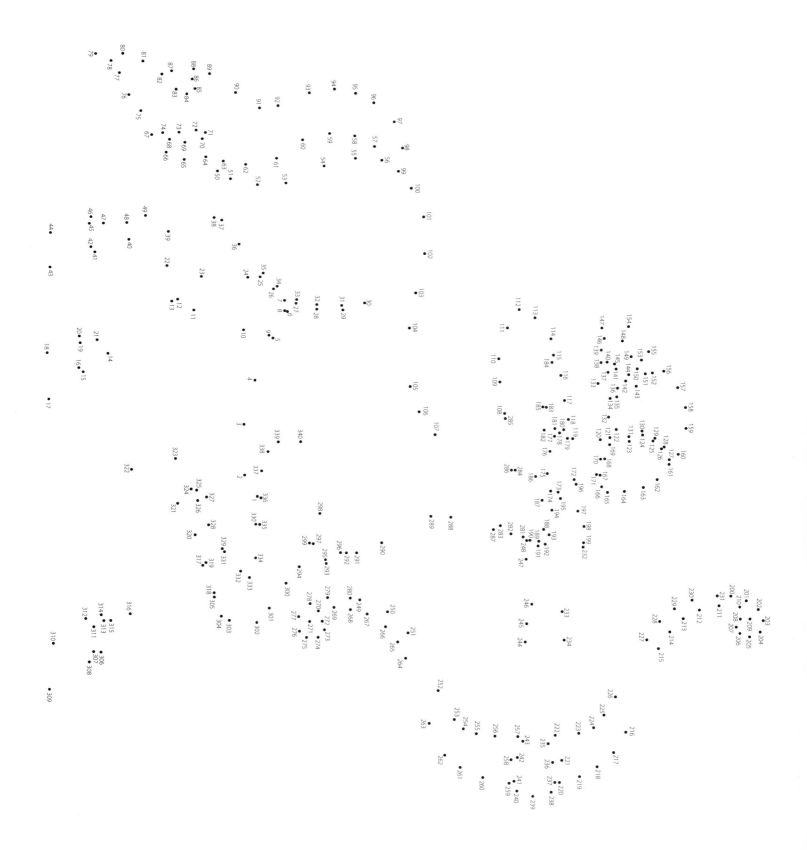

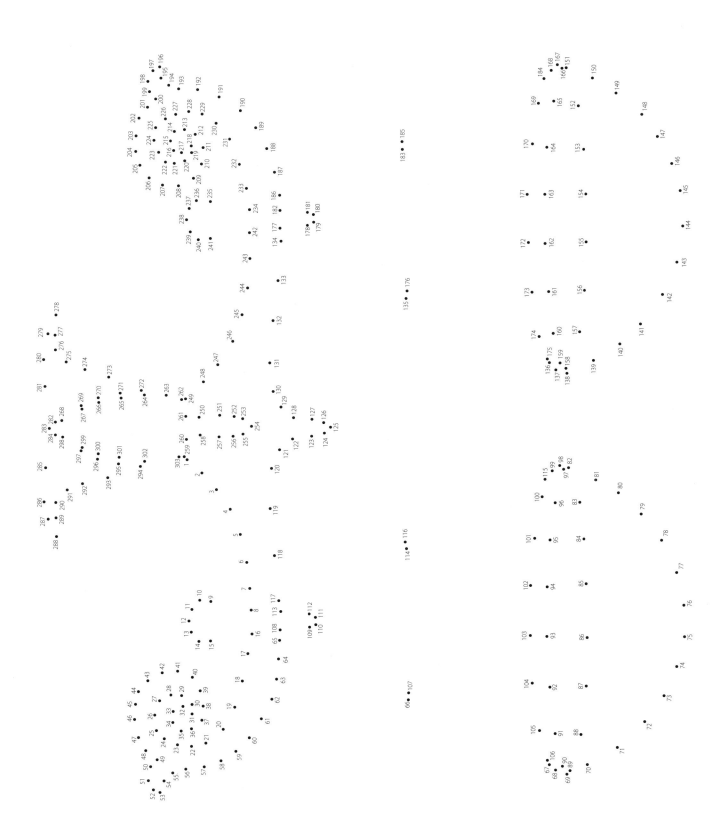

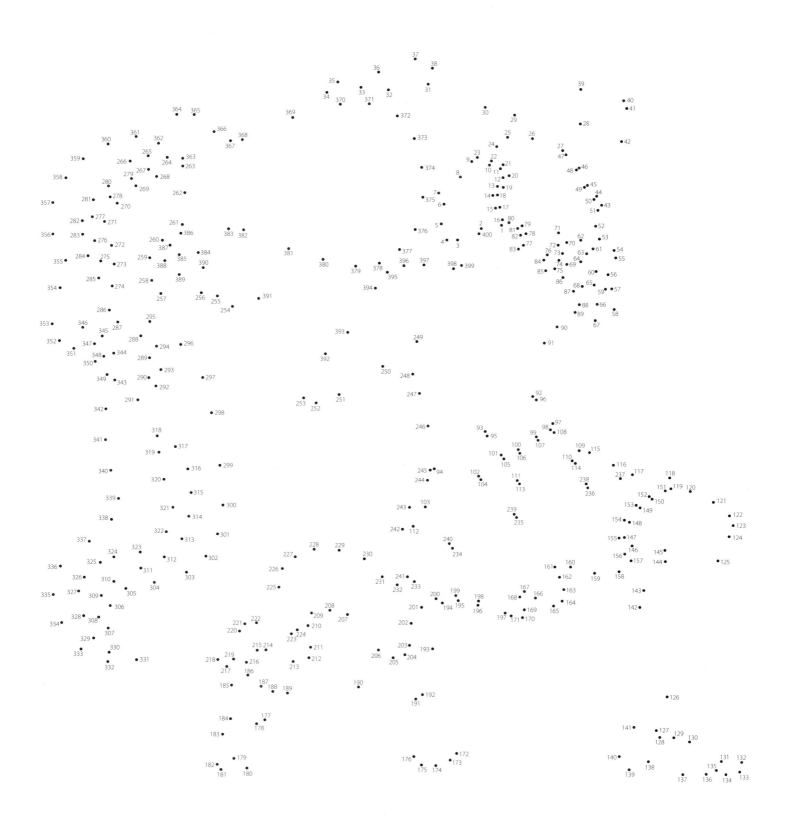

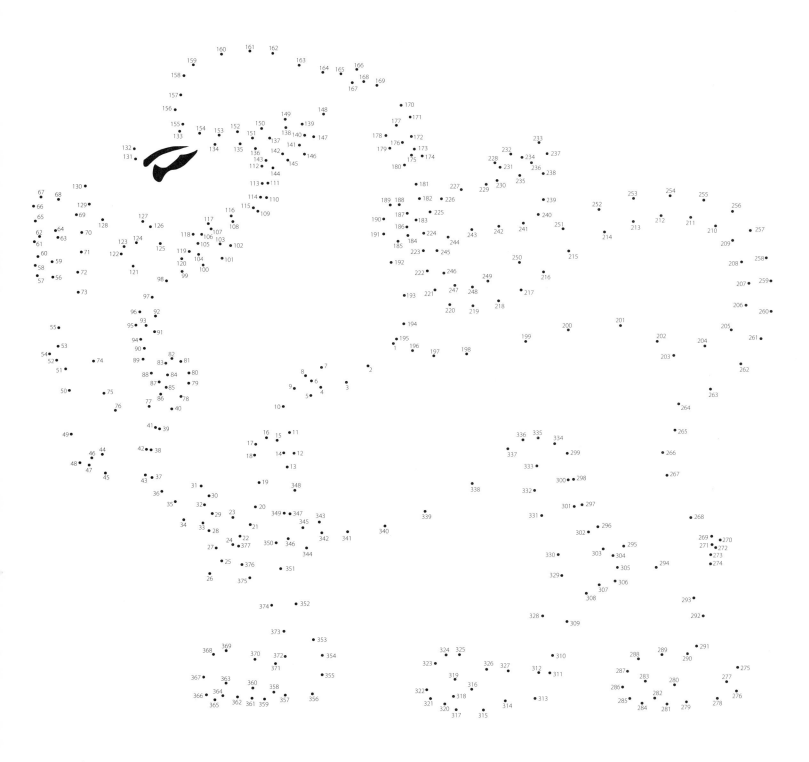

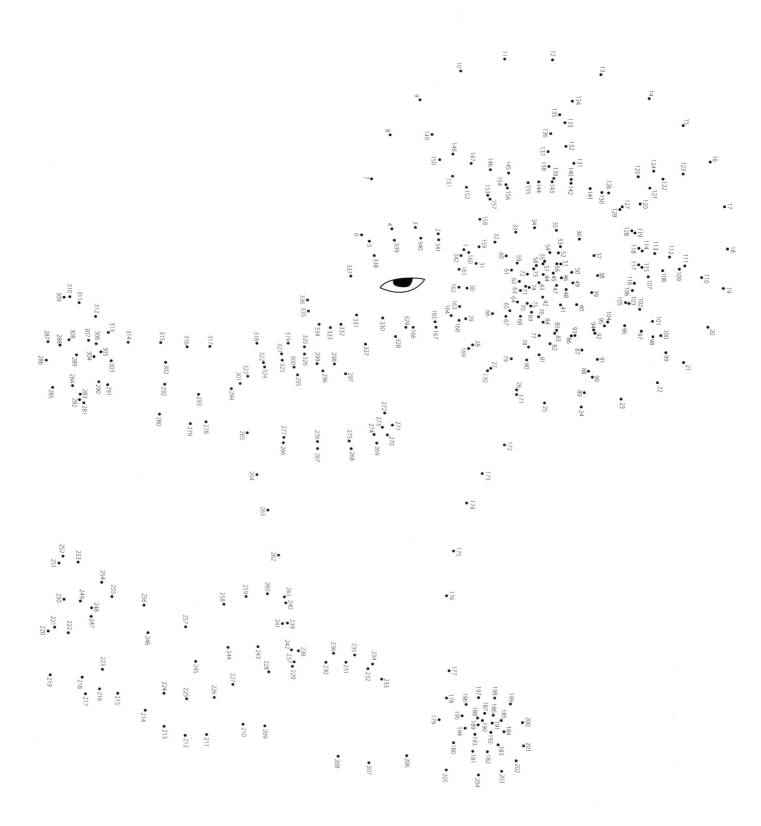

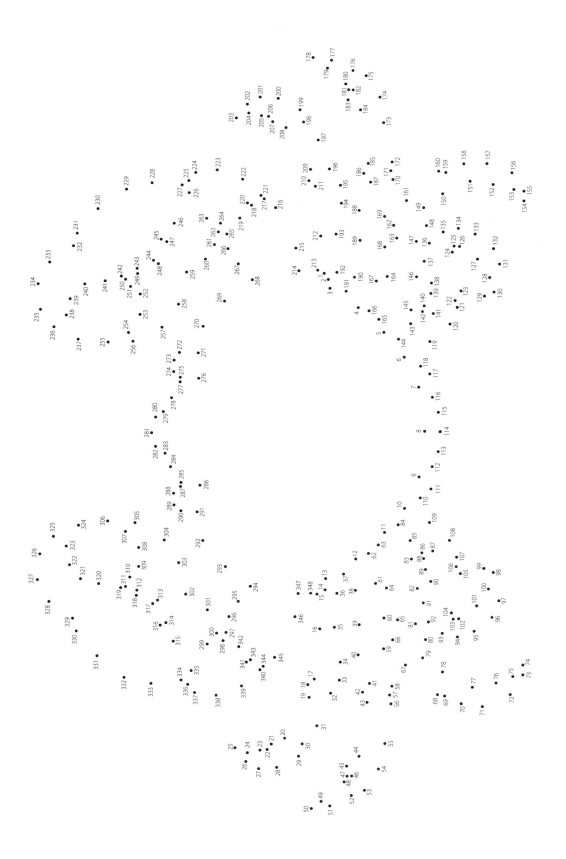

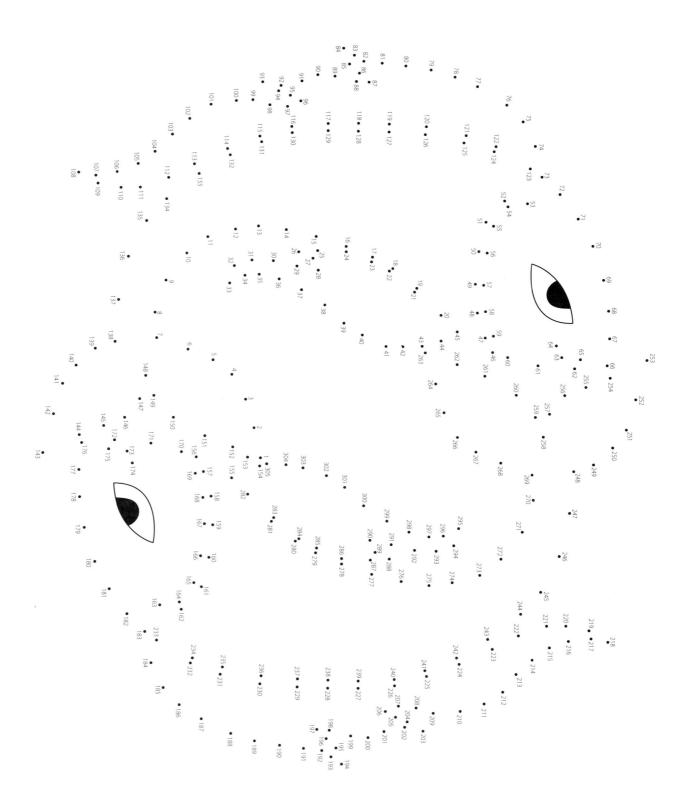

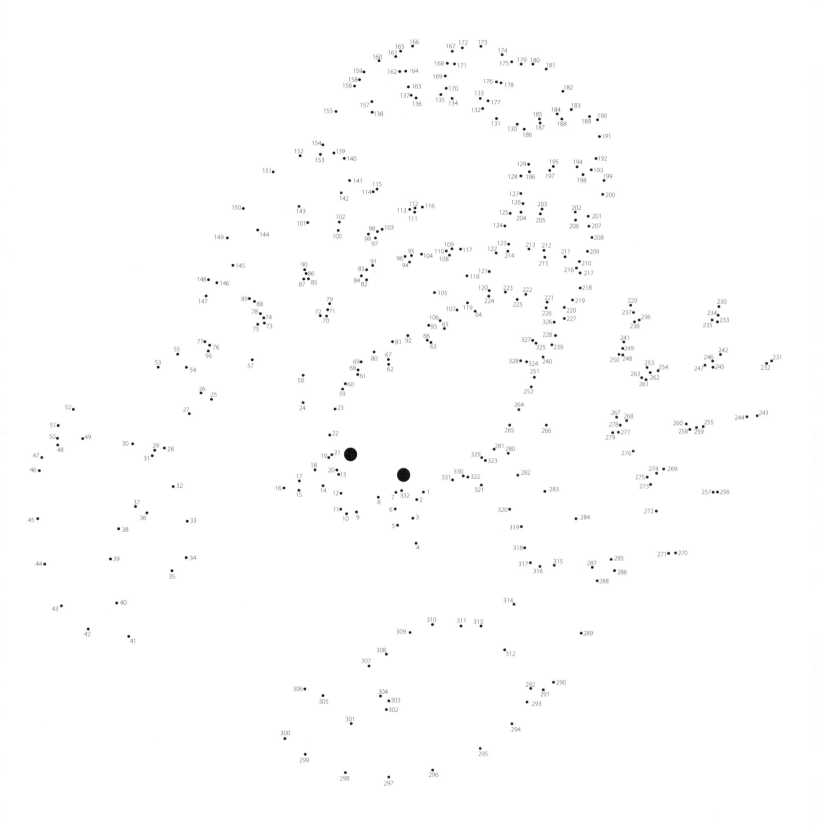

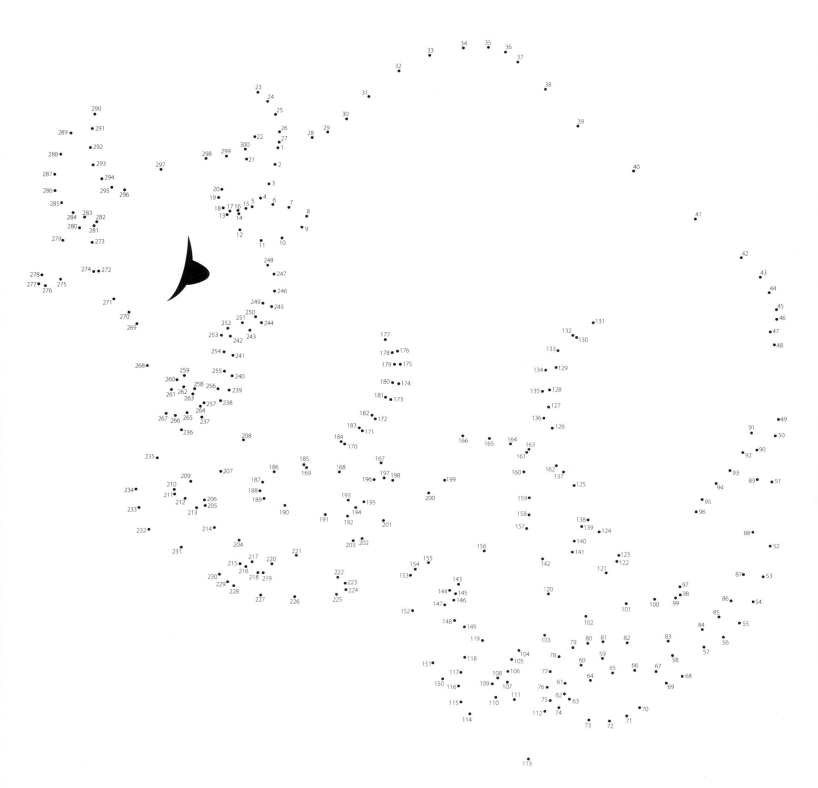

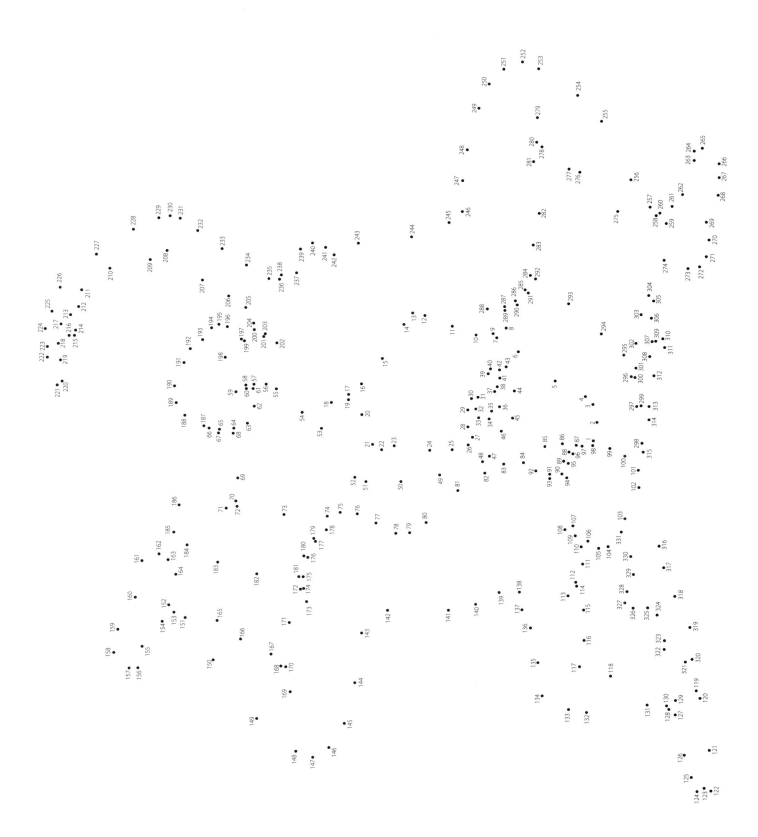

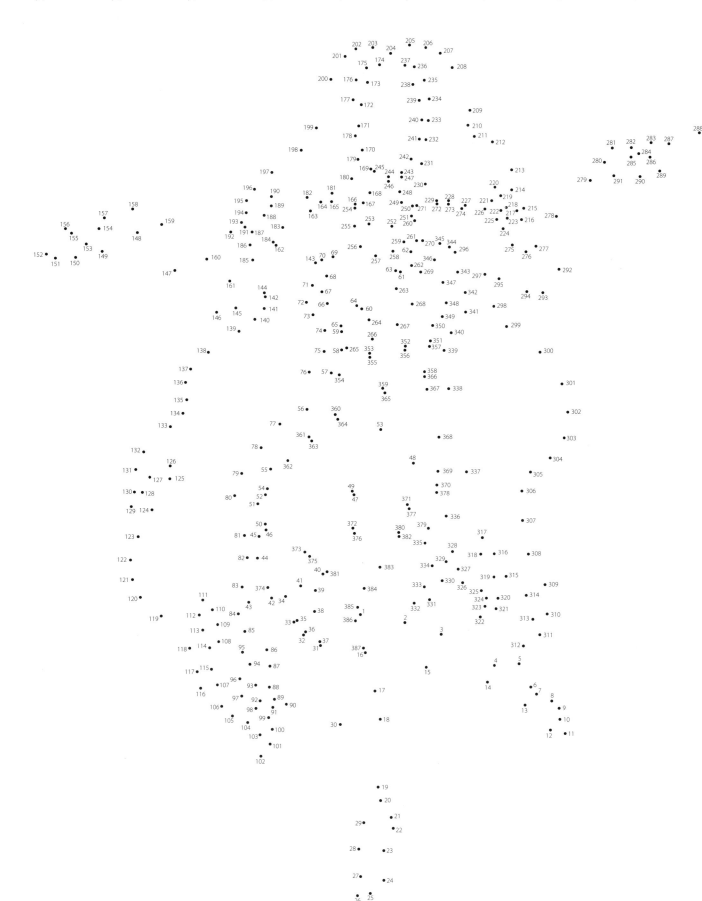

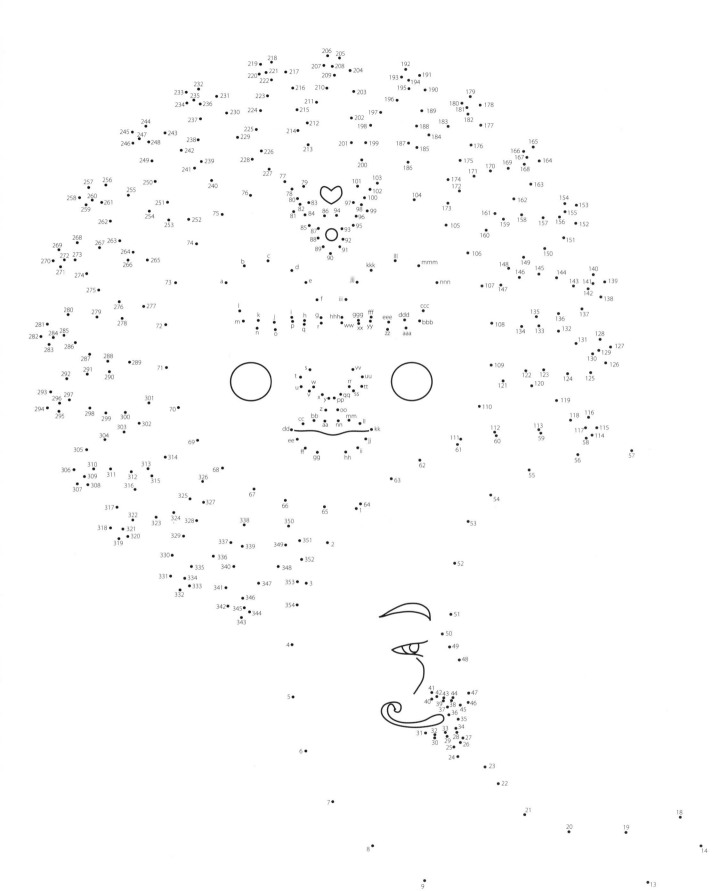

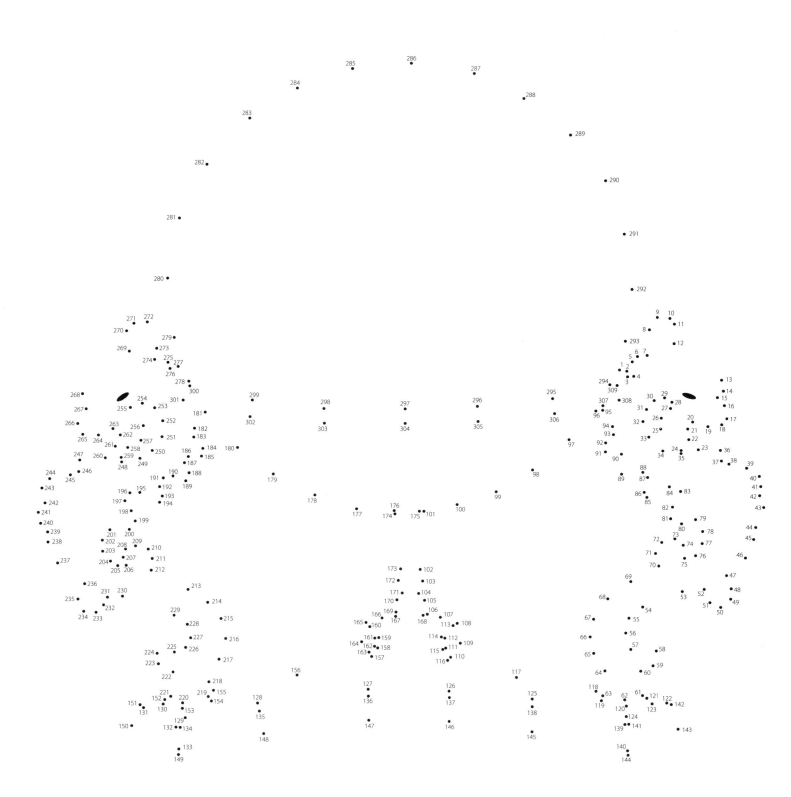

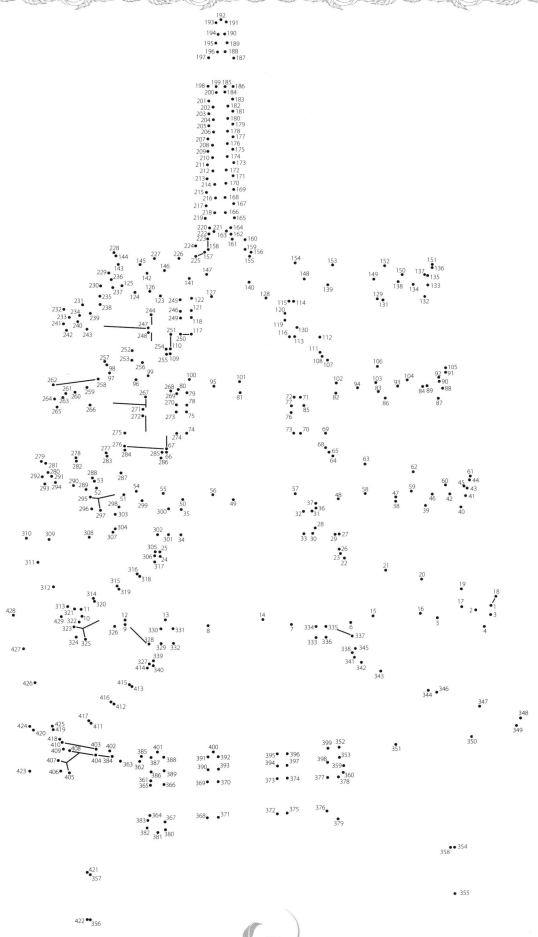

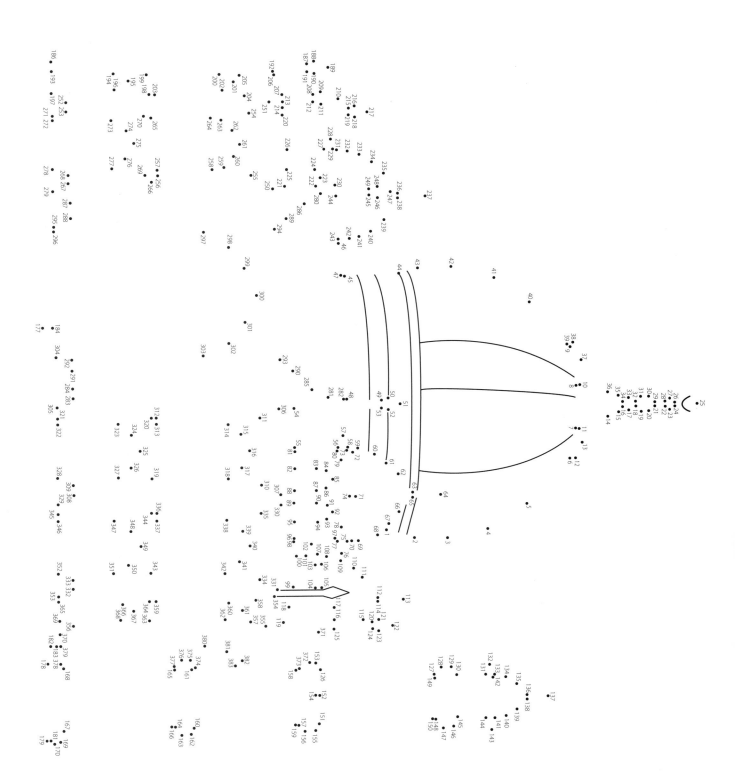

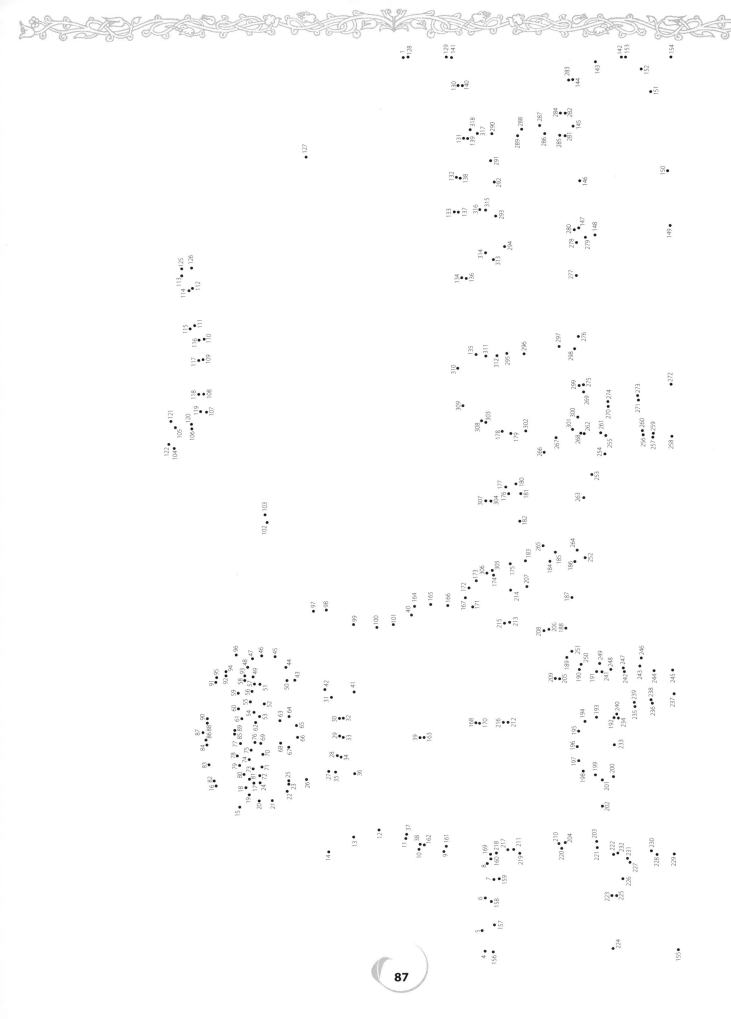

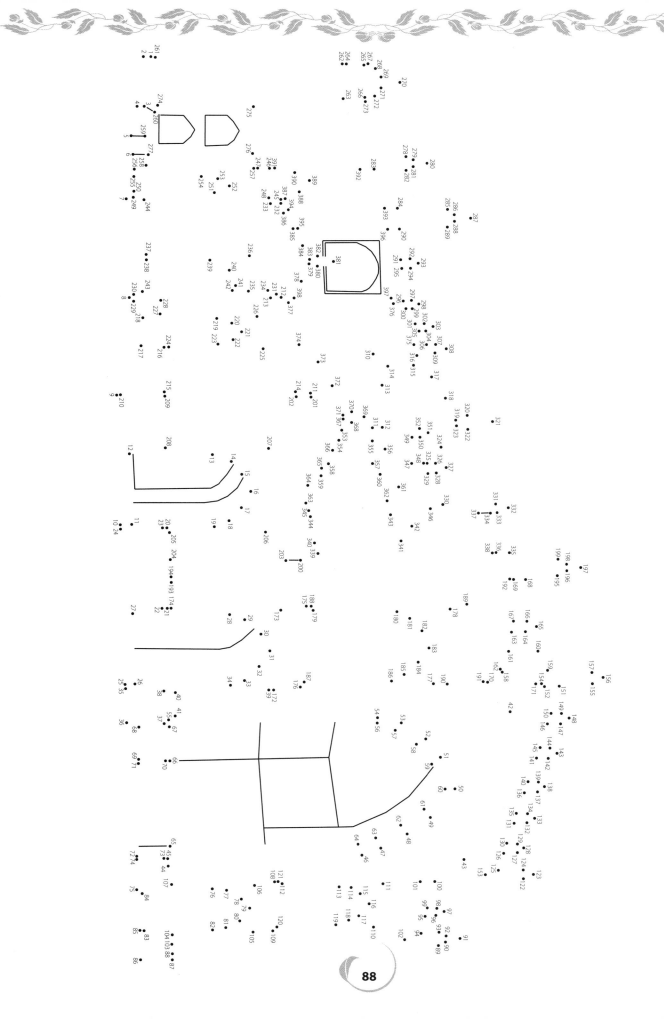

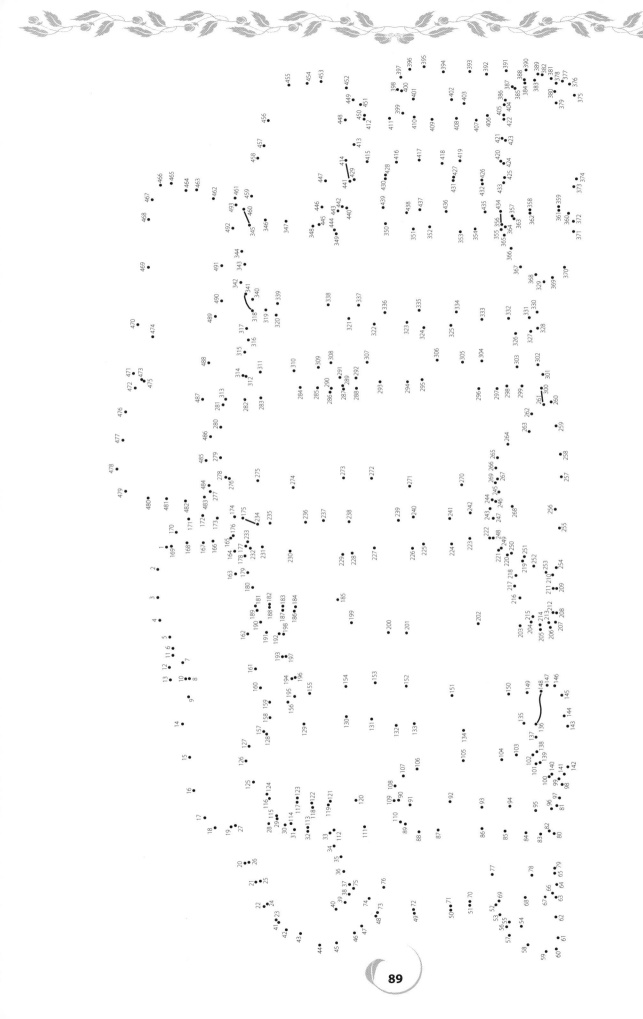

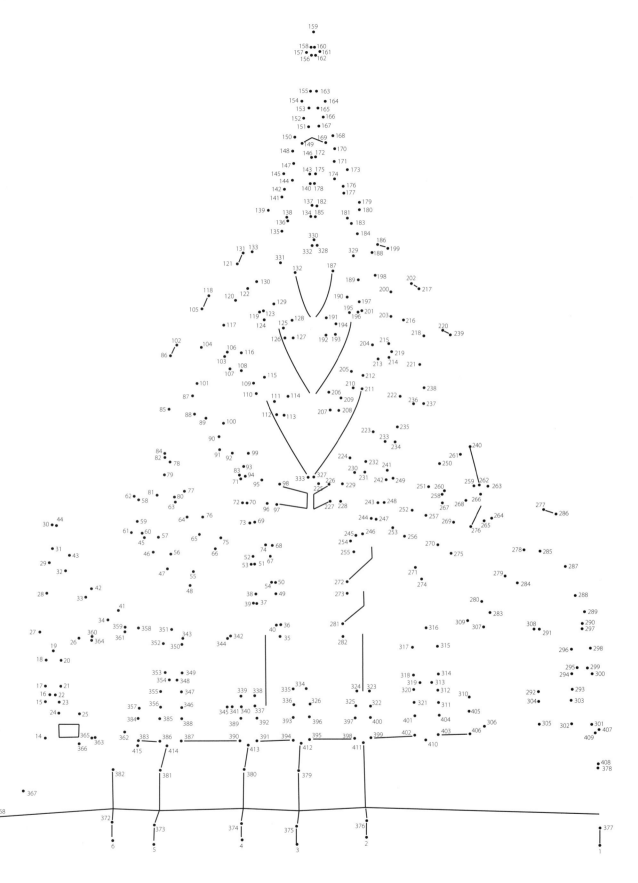

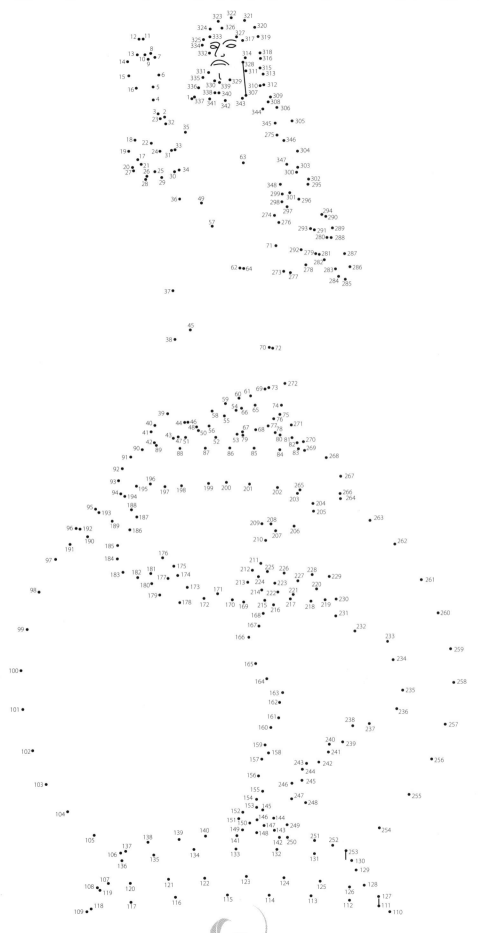

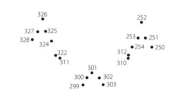

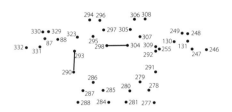

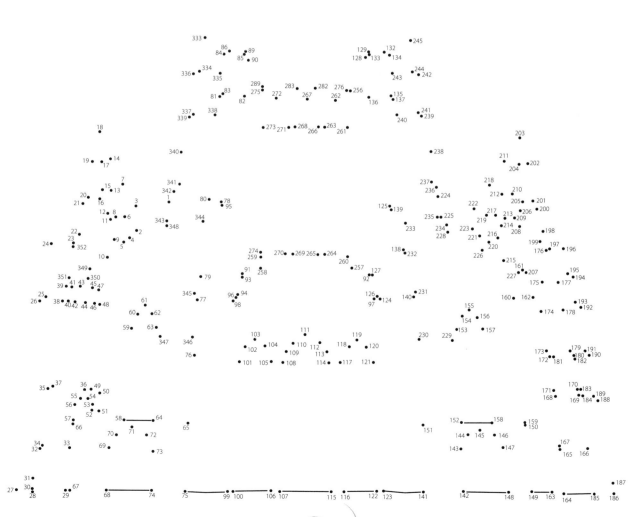

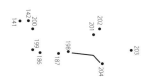
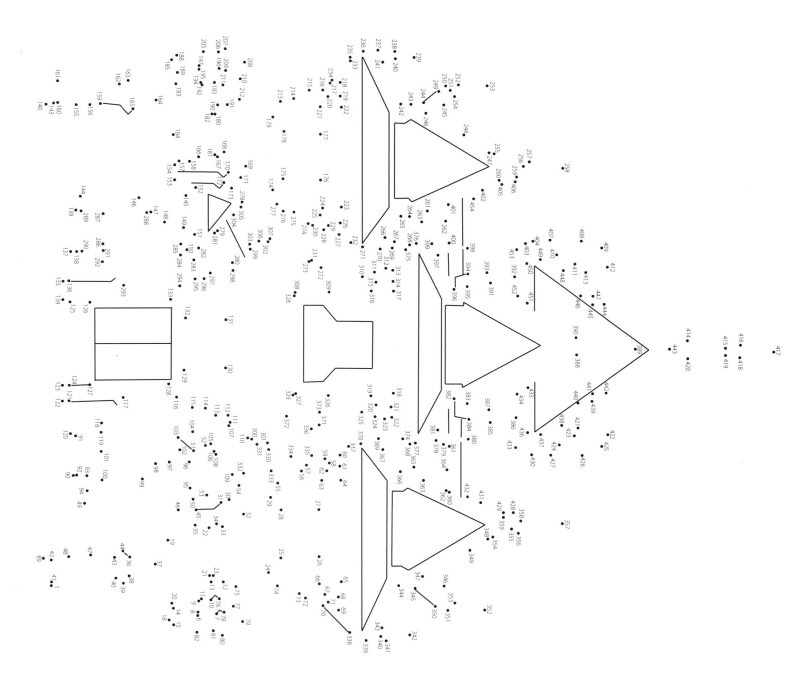

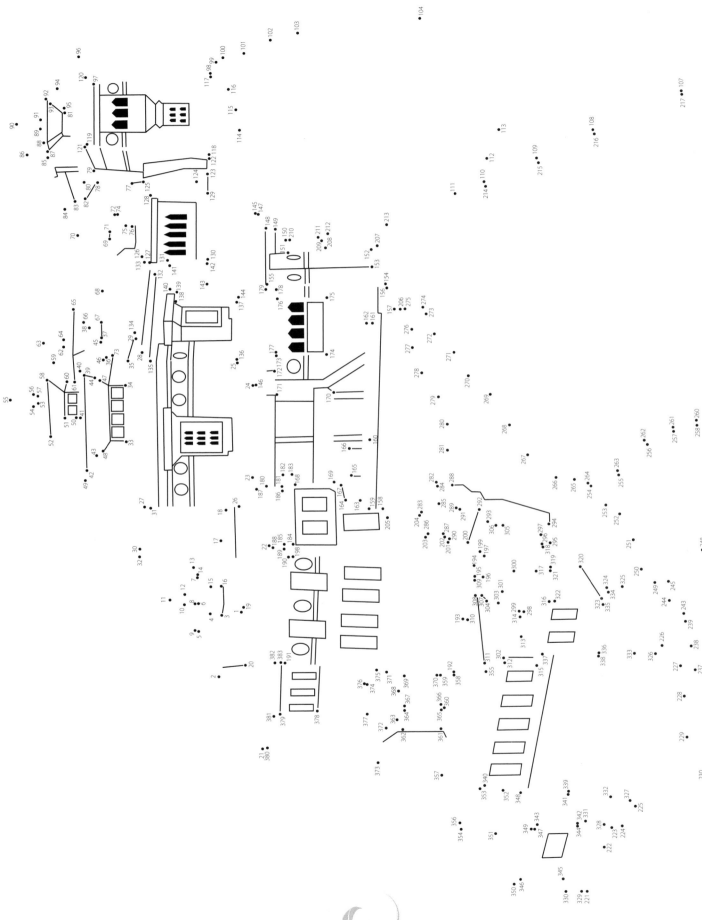

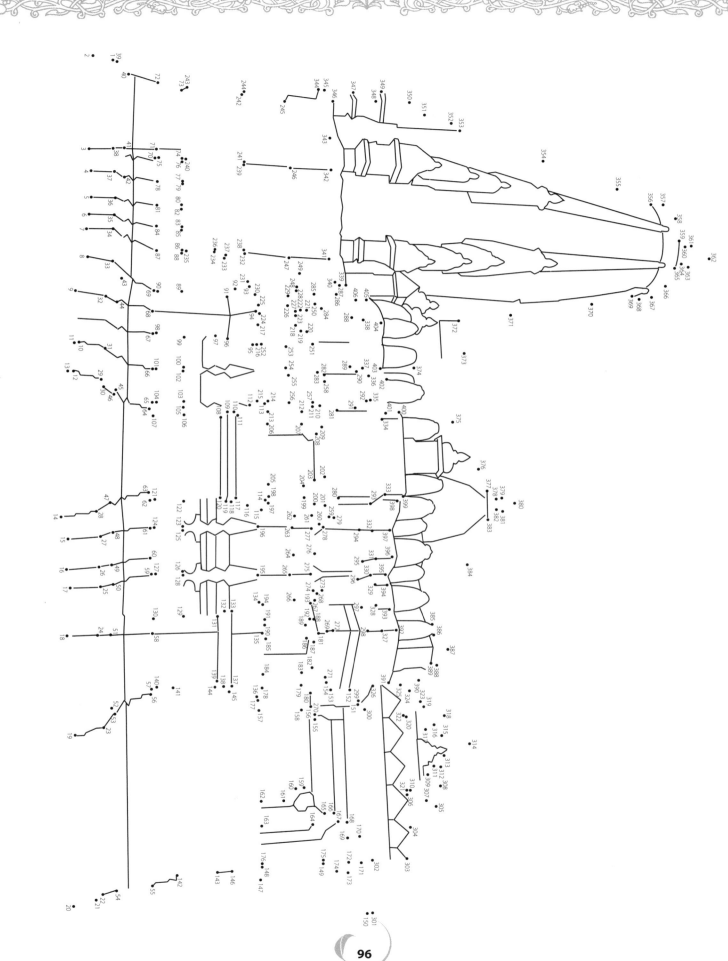

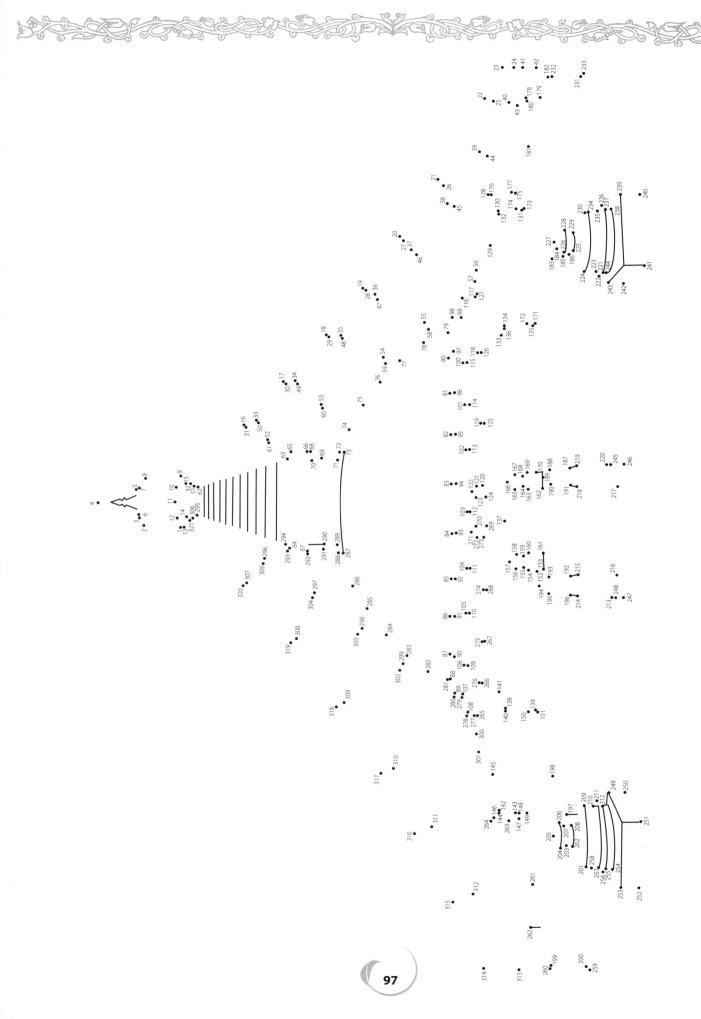

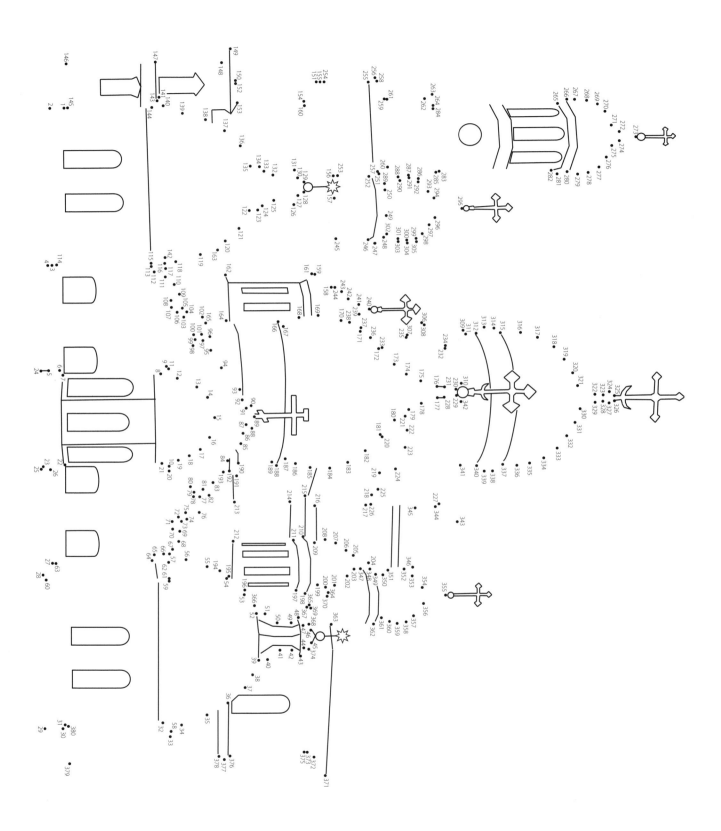

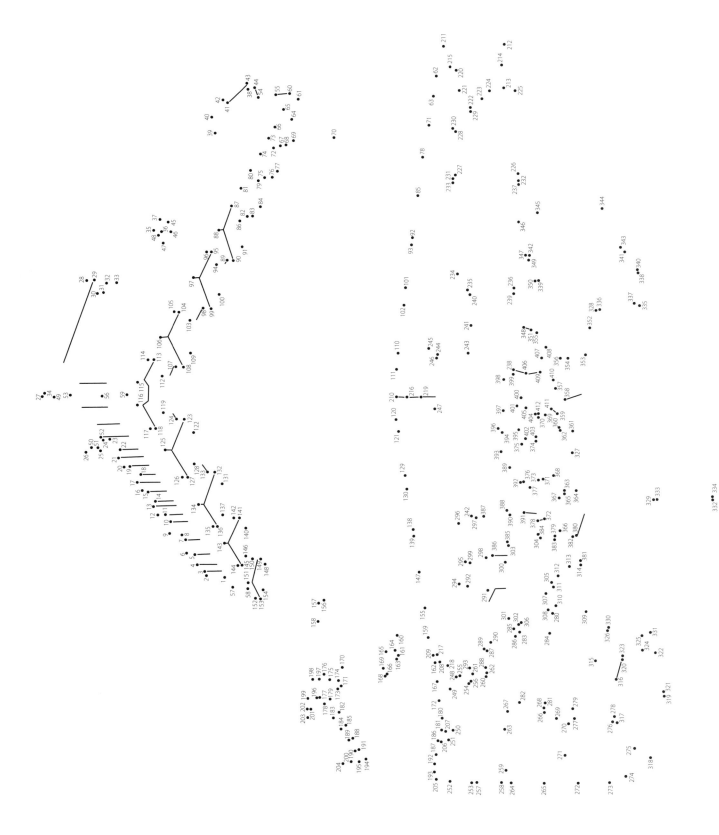

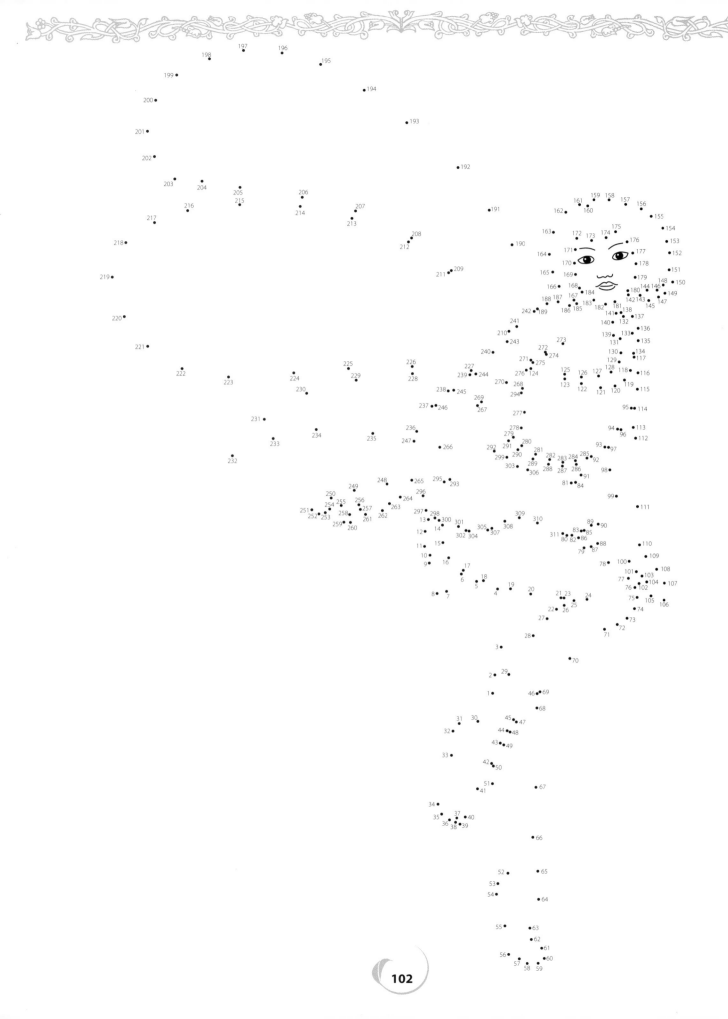

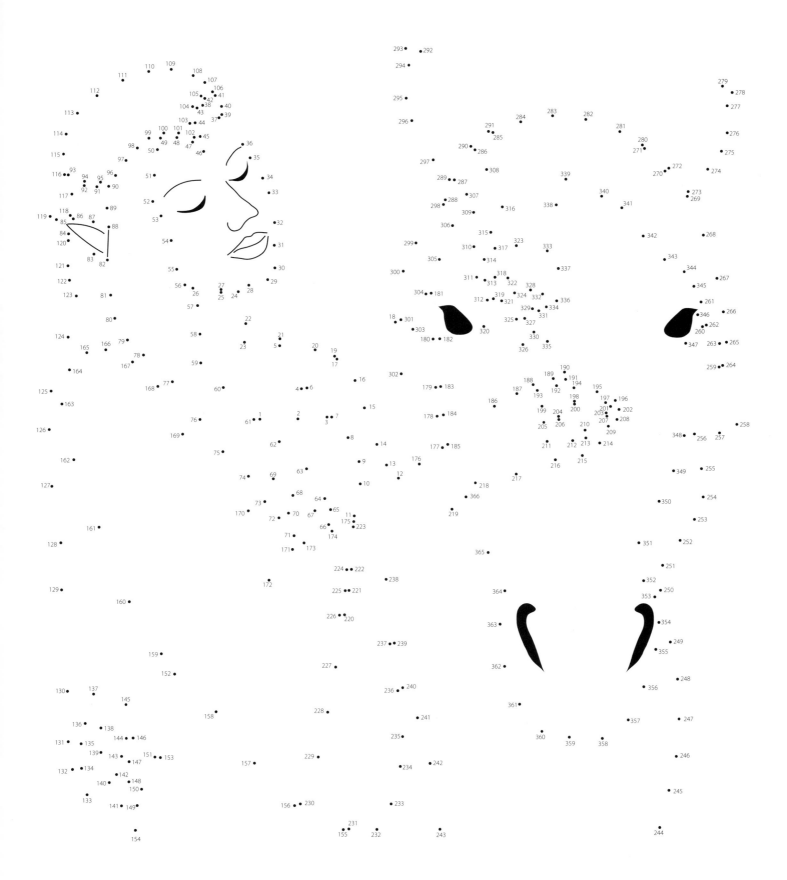

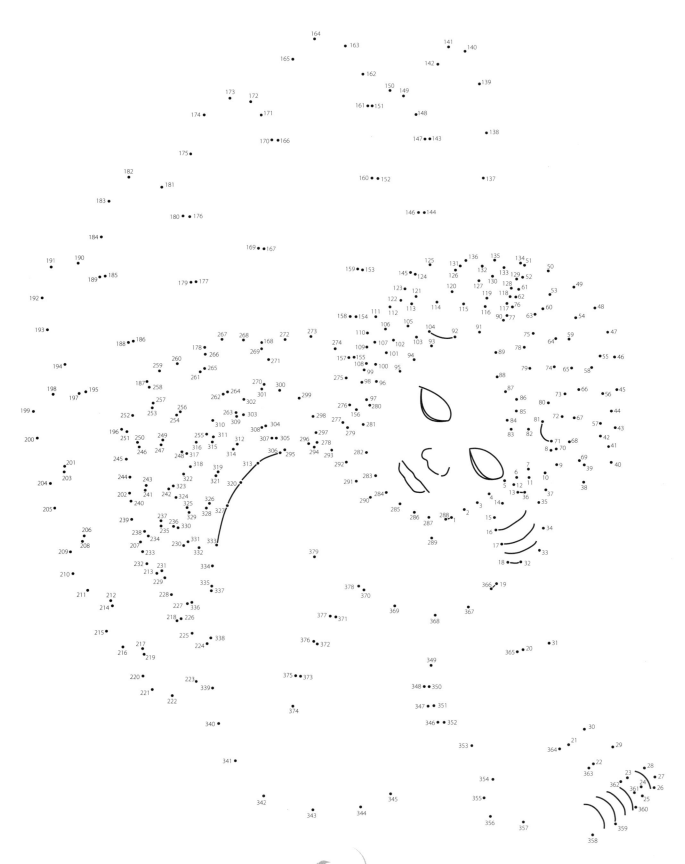

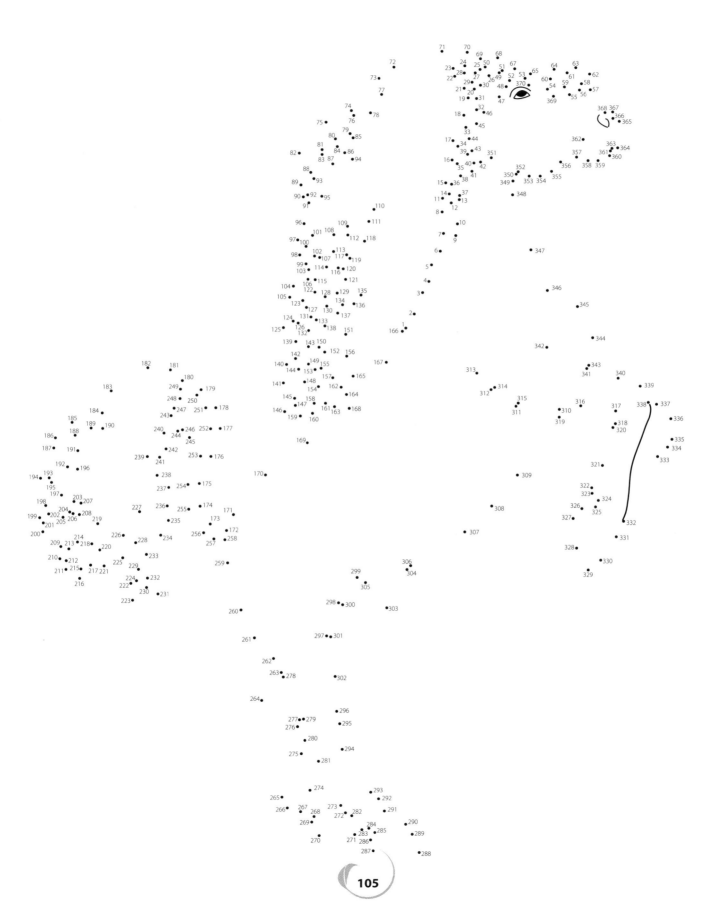

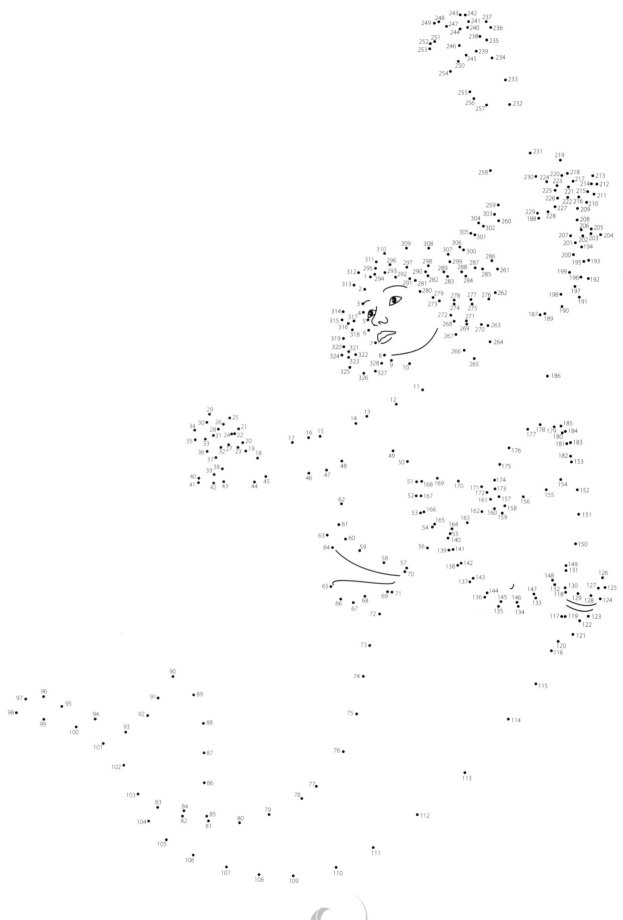

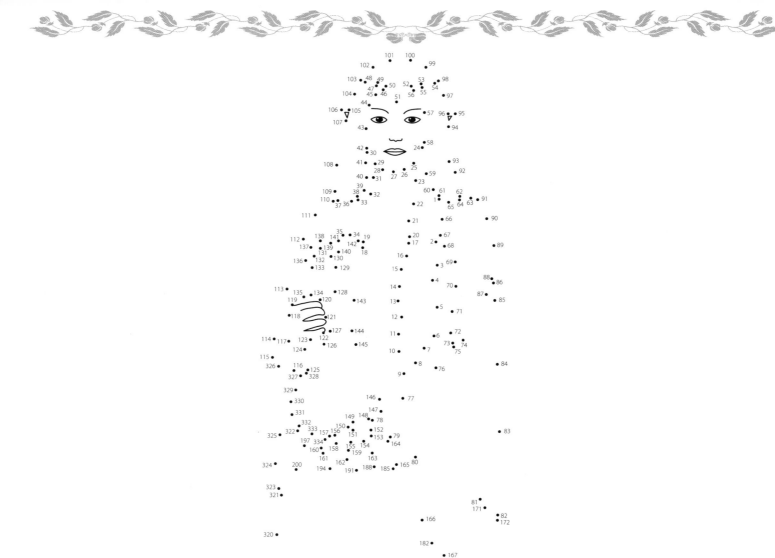
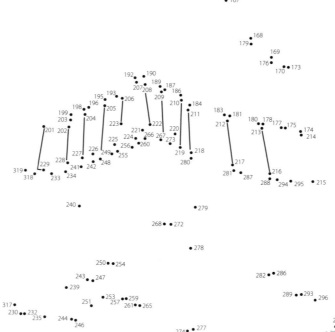

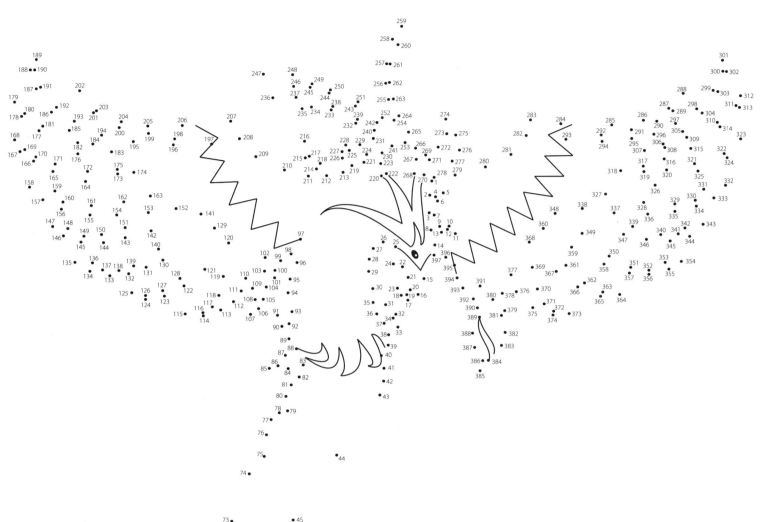

113

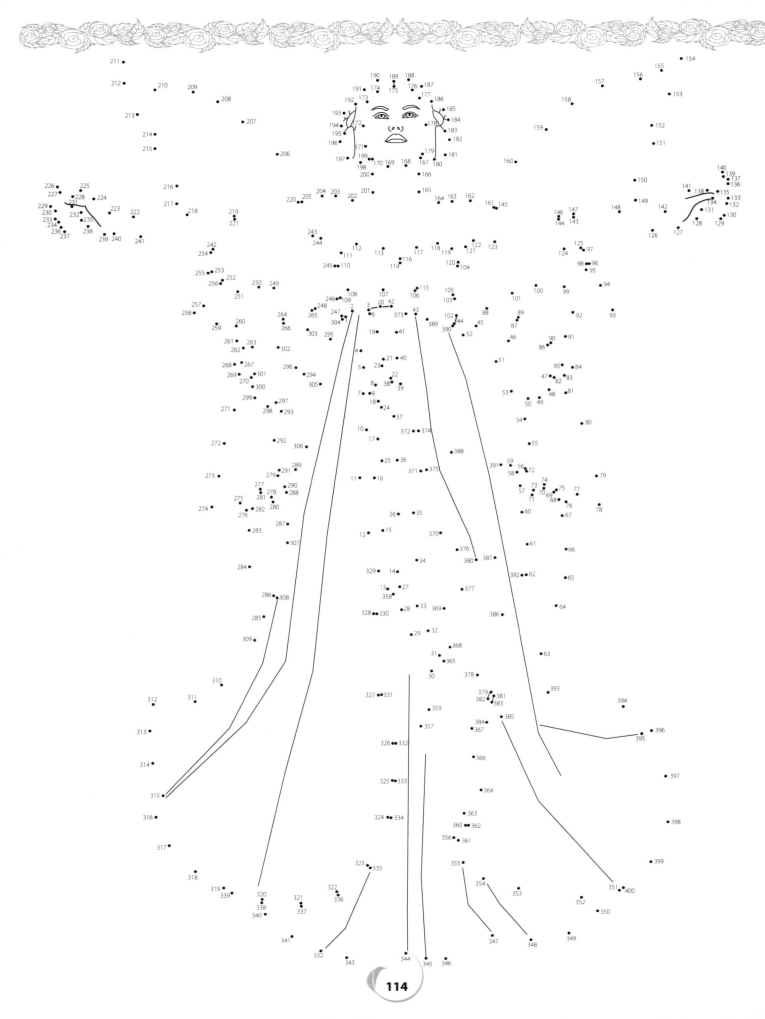

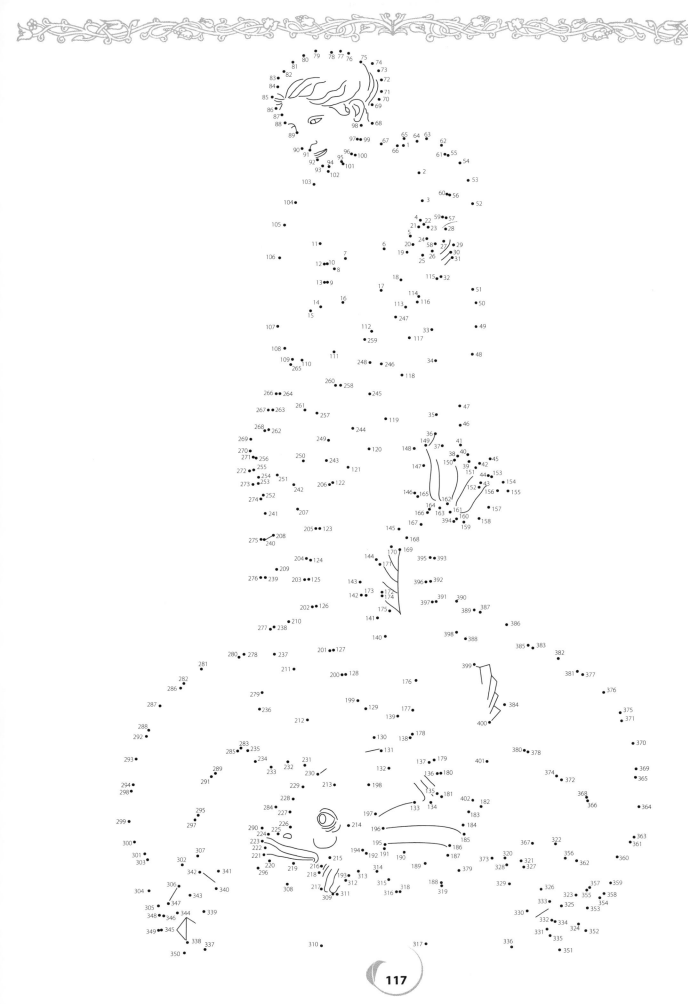

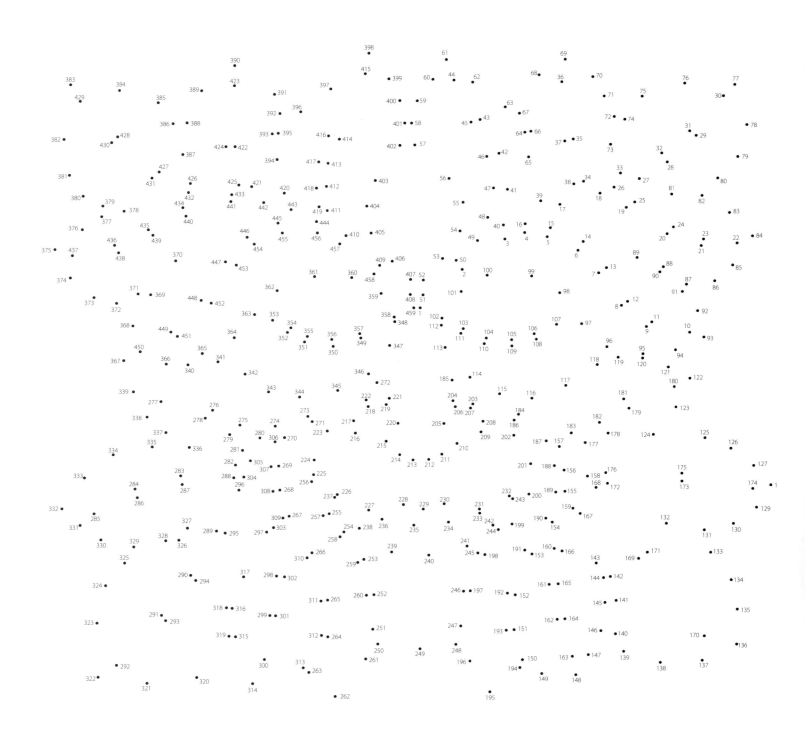

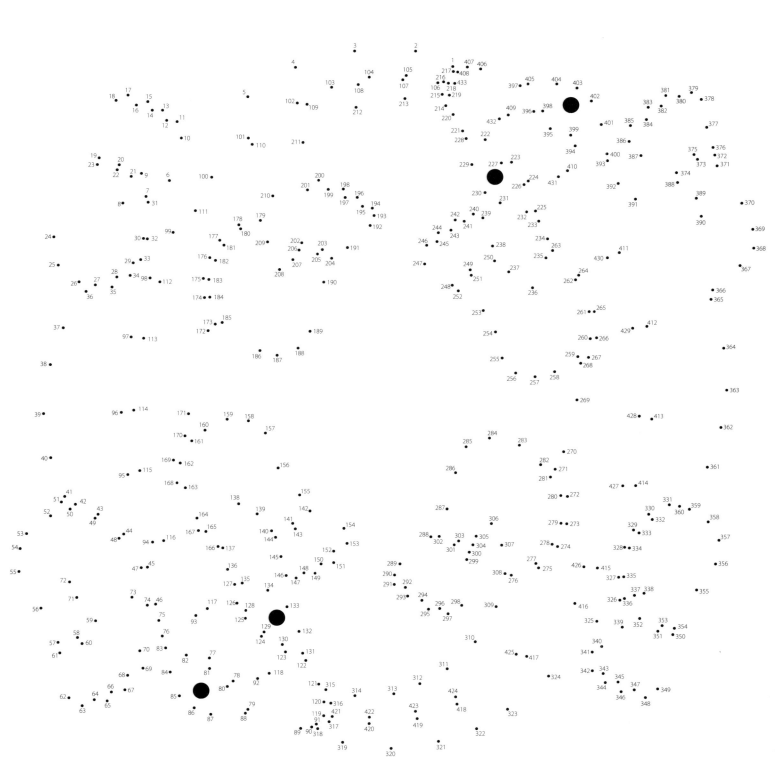

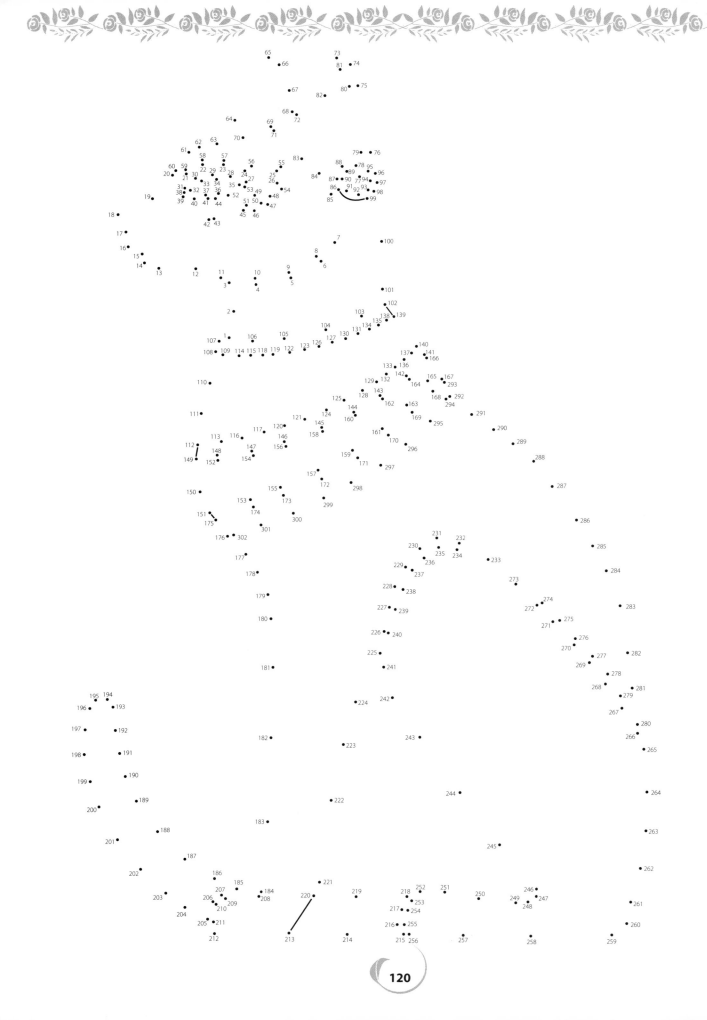

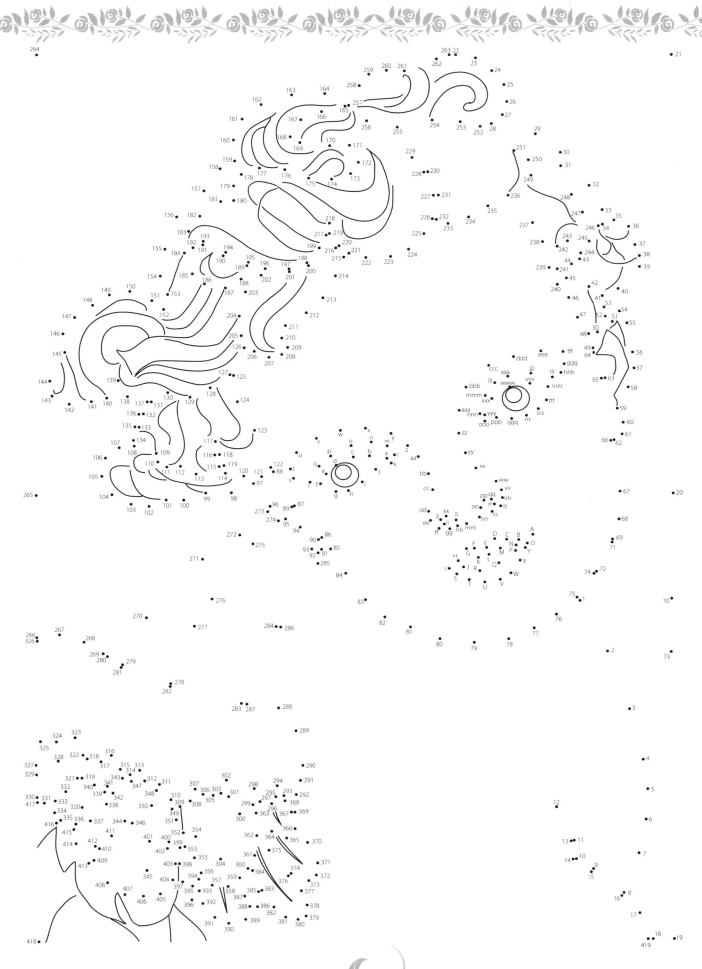

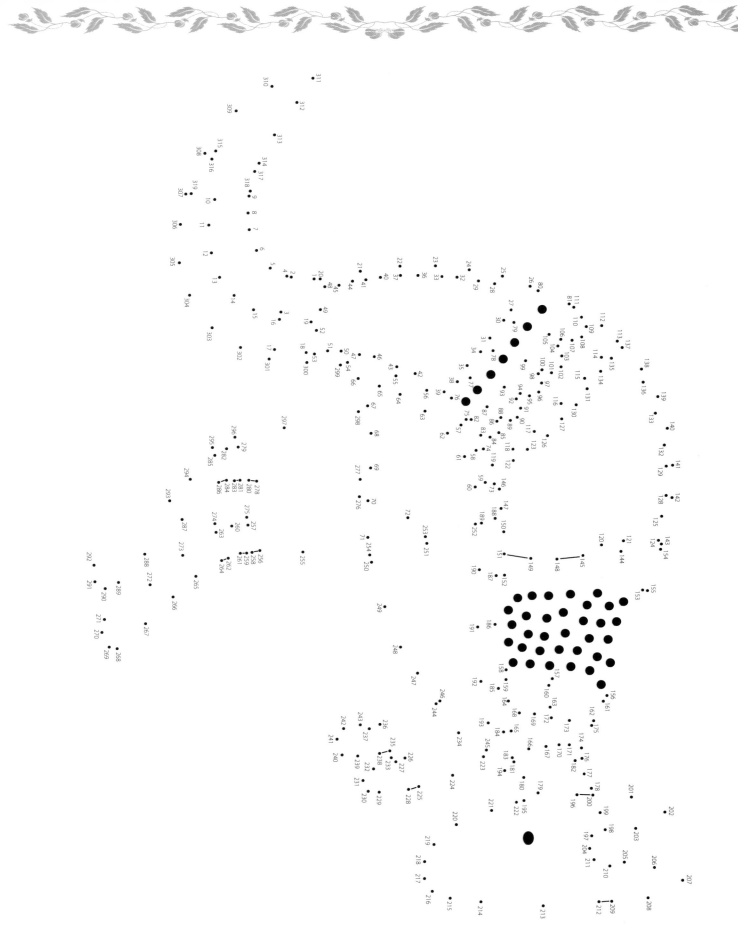

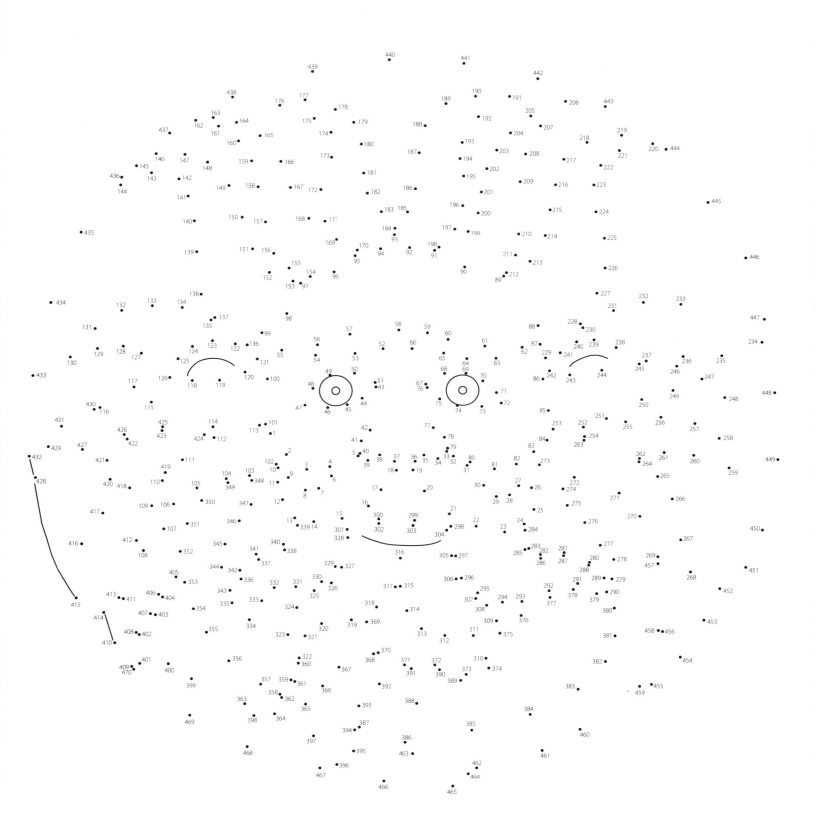

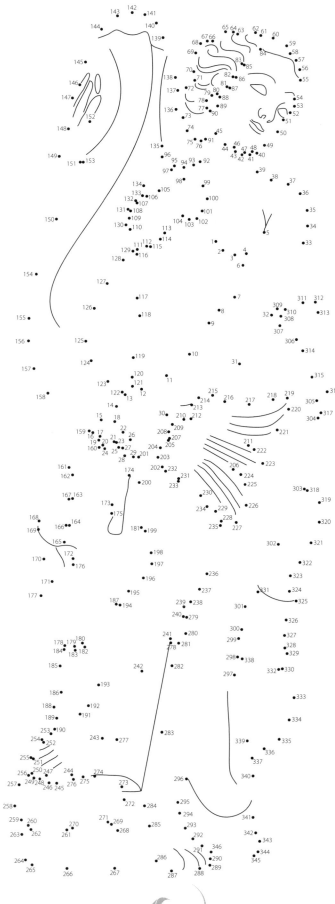

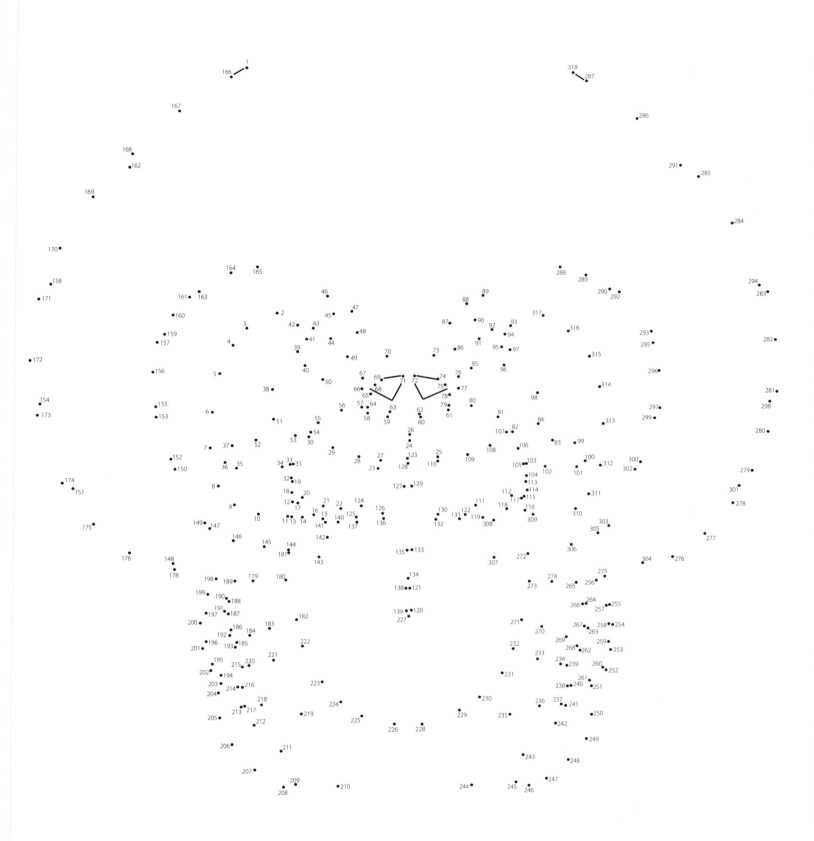

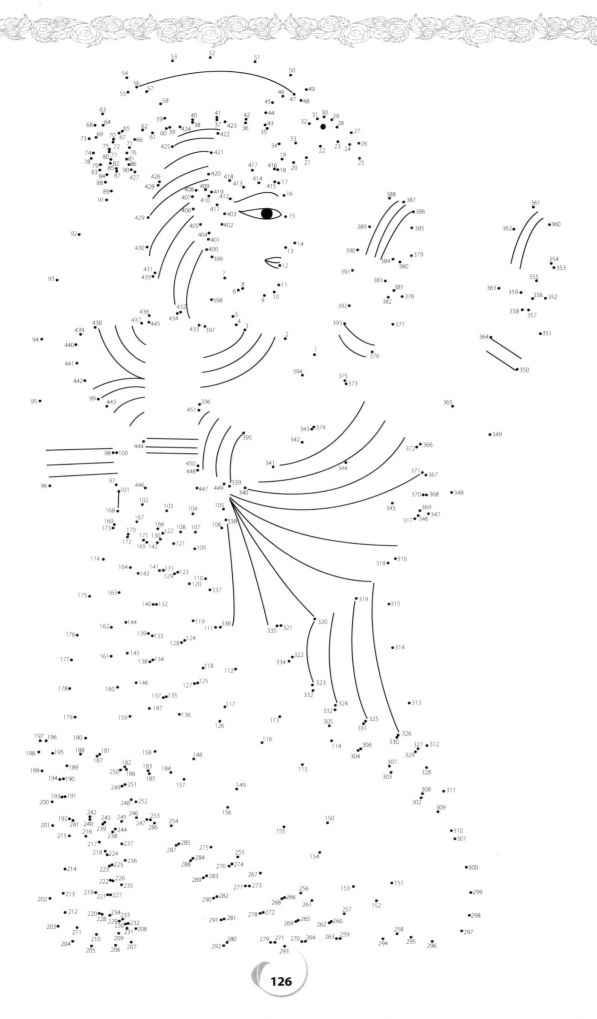

List of illustrations